Wonders of World Cultures

Exploring Africa

Interdisciplinary Readings and Activities

written and illustrated by

Toni Rhodes

J. WESTON
WALCH
PUBLISHER
Portland, Maine

About the Author

Toni Rhodes has a master's degree in education from Georgia State University, Atlanta, Georgia. She was a teacher in the Atlanta area for ten years. Currently, she is focusing on educational writing, especially in the area of history, which has been a lifelong interest. She writes a history-related children's column for a local newspaper and works in the Art History Department of Emory University, in Atlanta.

User's Guide
to
Walch Reproducible Books

As part of our general effort to provide educational materials which are as practical and economical as possible, we have designated this publication a "reproducible book." The designation means that purchase of the book includes purchase of the right to limited reproduction of all pages on which this symbol appears:

Here is the basic Walch policy: We grant to individual purchasers of this book the right to make sufficient copies of reproducible pages for use by all students of a single teacher. This permission is limited to a single teacher, and does not apply to entire schools or school systems, so institutions purchasing the book should pass the permission on to a single teacher. Copying of the book or its parts for resale is prohibited.

Any questions regarding this policy or requests to purchase further reproduction rights should be addressed to:

Permissions Editor
J. Weston Walch, Publisher
321 Valley Street • P. O. Box 658
Portland, Maine 04104-0658

1   2   3   4   5   6   7   8   9   10

ISBN 0-8251-3340-8

Contents

Section 1: Clues and Theories—Archaeological Wonders of Africa

Chapter 1: Nubia—Wonders in the Tumuli

Chapter 2: Great Zimbabwe—A Mystery and a Wonder

Section 2: Other Treasures and Wonders of African Cultures

Chapter 3: Fossil Wonders of Africa

Chapter 4: Rock Art Wonders of the Bushmen

Introduction

This book focuses on the history and cultures of Africa. The history of Egypt, however, is mainly covered in the book *Wonders of World Cultures—Exploring the Near and Middle East.*

Each chapter tells a story of a cultural "treasure" or "wonder" of Africa. Section 1 focuses on the interpretation of archaeological artifacts such as the rock walls of Great Zimbabwe. These artifacts are the "clues" that lead to theories about how ancient people lived and worked. Students are invited to play the role of archaeologist and to think of theories based on clues provided in the chapters.

Section II focuses on other cultural wonders of Africa and are presented in a straight-forward, narrative format.

Activities in each chapter provide opportunities for students to learn more about the culture that each wonder comes from. Many of the activities engage the students in experiential and interdisciplinary learning—instructional practices recommended by the National Council for the Social Studies in its report "Social Studies in the Middle School: A Report of the Task Force on Social Studies in the Middle School" (approved by NCSS Board of Directors, January 1991).

In the report, the NCSS recommends experiential learning because "all of us learn by doing. It follows, therefore, that middle level students benefit from concrete experiences such as role-playing, interviewing, community service, and similar activities in which they are able to analyze a common experience and explore ideas and values." The report states that interdisciplinary instruction focuses upon a central theme and draws from two or more subject areas. "The skills and knowledge gained from study involving a variety of disciplines enhance the social studies program as well as other parts of the curriculum."

It is hoped that you and your students will learn more about the wonders of our world's cultures through these readings and activities. Enjoy them!

General Outline of This Book

I. Time Line

The time line shows the dates and events included in each chapter. You can copy the time line for students to refer to as they read.

II. Internet Sites

This page includes a list of Internet sites that are relevant to Africa.

III. Introductory "Clues and Theories" Activity

Introduce your students to the field of archaeology by taking them through the activity on page *ix*. The goal is to help students see that objects from the past (**clues**) can tell about people and cultures in history (**theories**). Students will sharpen their skills in determining relevance of information and drawing conclusions. They will practice communicating their theories and backing them up with clues. This will provide some practice for Section 1, where they read about and then draw their own conclusions about archeological discoveries.

IV. Chapters:

A. Teacher Guide Pages

- Provide a chapter summary, which defines the "wonder" in the chapter and lists major themes covered in the chapter.

- Give answers to "Think About It" questions contained in chapter reading.

- Give answers to "Your Theory" questions contained in Section 1 chapter readings.

- Give answers to activities that require specific answers. (Most activities are open-ended.)

- Give answers to "Thought/Discussion Questions."

- Include a bibliography, including adult and juvenile books and magazine articles.

B. Reading about a "Treasure" or "Wonder" Centered in Africa

- A general map of the area and a focus map showing the specific area covered in the reading are included.

Section 1: Archaeological Wonders (artifacts)

- "Think About It" questions in the reading help students reflect on the material.

- "Your Theory" boxes let students take on the role of archaeologist.

Section 2: Other Treasures and Wonders of African Cultures (expands the concept)

- "Think About It" questions in the reading help students reflect on the material.

C. Activities to Enhance Students' Understanding

- Many activities are "hands-on" and give students a chance to learn by doing.

- If students do all activities within each chapter, they will use skills and knowledge from at least two disciplines.

- Activities include: step-by-step instructions, objectives, time and materials needed to complete activity, suggested number of students, ways to extend or adapt activities.

D. Thought/Discussion Questions to Enhance Students' Understanding

- These questions can be used as an individual activity or for group discussion after students complete the reading.

- These questions help students focus and expand on information in the chapter.

Time Line of Dates

from Chapters in this Book

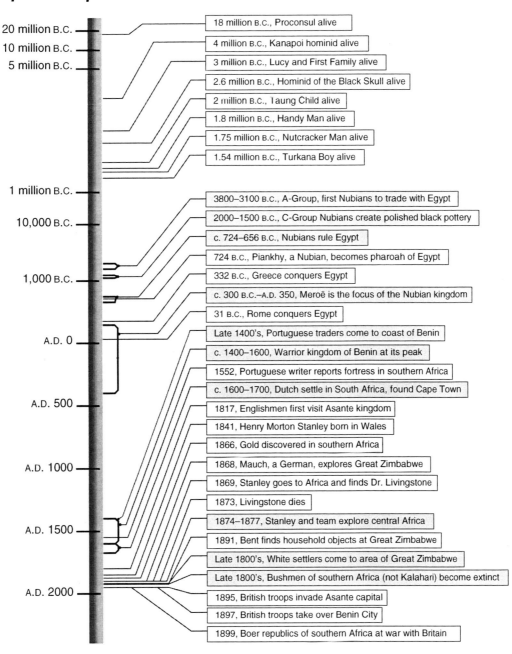

20 million B.C.	18 million B.C., Proconsul alive
10 million B.C.	4 million B.C., Kanapoi hominid alive
5 million B.C.	3 million B.C., Lucy and First Family alive
	2.6 million B.C., Hominid of the Black Skull alive
	2 million B.C., Taung Child alive
	1.8 million B.C., Handy Man alive
	1.75 million B.C., Nutcracker Man alive
	1.54 million B.C., Turkana Boy alive
1 million B.C.	3800–3100 B.C., A-Group, first Nubians to trade with Egypt
10,000 B.C.	2000–1500 B.C., C-Group Nubians create polished black pottery
	c. 724–656 B.C., Nubians rule Egypt
	724 B.C., Piankhy, a Nubian, becomes pharoah of Egypt
1,000 B.C.	332 B.C., Greece conquers Egypt
	c. 300 B.C.–A.D. 350, Meroë is the focus of the Nubian kingdom
	31 B.C., Rome conquers Egypt
A.D. 0	Late 1400's, Portuguese traders come to coast of Benin
	c. 1400–1600, Warrior kingdom of Benin at its peak
	1552, Portuguese writer reports fortress in southern Africa
	c. 1600–1700, Dutch settle in South Africa, found Cape Town
A.D. 500	1817, Englishmen first visit Asante kingdom
	1841, Henry Morton Stanley born in Wales
	1866, Gold discovered in southern Africa
A.D. 1000	1868, Mauch, a German, explores Great Zimbabwe
	1869, Stanley goes to Africa and finds Dr. Livingstone
	1873, Livingstone dies
	1874–1877, Stanley and team explore central Africa
A.D. 1500	1891, Bent finds household objects at Great Zimbabwe
	Late 1800's, White settlers come to area of Great Zimbabwe
	Late 1800's, Bushmen of southern Africa (not Kalahari) become extinct
A.D. 2000	1895, British troops invade Asante capital
	1897, British troops take over Benin City
	1899, Boer republics of southern Africa at war with Britain

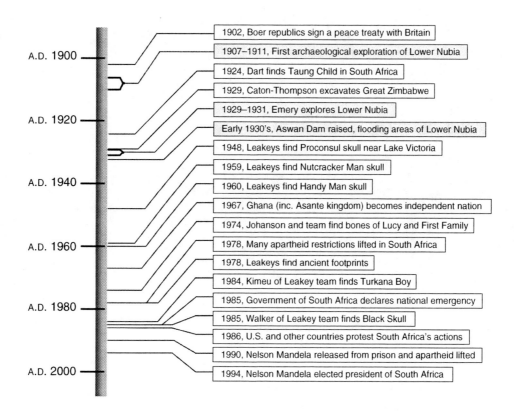

A.D. 1900 — 1902, Boer republics sign a peace treaty with Britain

1907–1911, First archaeological exploration of Lower Nubia

1924, Dart finds Taung Child in South Africa

1929, Caton-Thompson excavates Great Zimbabwe

A.D. 1920 — 1929–1931, Emery explores Lower Nubia

Early 1930's, Aswan Dam raised, flooding areas of Lower Nubia

1948, Leakeys find Proconsul skull near Lake Victoria

1959, Leakeys find Nutcracker Man skull

A.D. 1940 — 1960, Leakeys find Handy Man skull

1967, Ghana (inc. Asante kingdom) becomes independent nation

1974, Johanson and team find bones of Lucy and First Family

A.D. 1960 — 1978, Many apartheid restrictions lifted in South Africa

1978, Leakeys find ancient footprints

1984, Kimeu of Leakey team finds Turkana Boy

1985, Government of South Africa declares national emergency

A.D. 1980 — 1985, Walker of Leakey team finds Black Skull

1986, U.S. and other countries protest South Africa's actions

1990, Nelson Mandela released from prison and apartheid lifted

A.D. 2000 — 1994, Nelson Mandela elected president of South Africa

Internet Sites

Please keep in mind that Internet sites change constantly; therefore, the ones listed below may have moved or changed since the printing of this book. These sites were chosen because of their potential to be permanent sites on the Internet and because of their established credentials.

General Interest—Africa

Rice Archaeology—Rice University
www.ruf.rice.edu/~anth/arch/mali-interactive/index.html

Focuses on the archaeological site of Jenne-jeno in western Africa (present-day Mali).

Includes:

◆ maps
◆ photos of artifacts
◆ biographies of archaeologists and their children
◆ summary of findings at Jenne-jeno
◆ on-site journal of sixth-grade son of archaeologists
◆ teaching resources

"Odyssey Online" by the Carlos Museum of Emory University, Atlanta, Georgia
www.emory.edu/CARLOS/

◆ Photos and descriptions of artifacts from sub-Saharan Africa

South Africa

"Die Burger"
www.naspers.co.za/dieburger/

This is a daily newspaper in Afrikaans and English.

"African National Congress"
www.anc.org.za/

The African National Congress is the majority political party in the South African government (as of this writing). This site contains information about the government, established in 1994 after the first democratic elections. The text of government documents and information about President Mandela is also included.

Nubia

"Kelsey Museum of Archaeology"
www.umich.edu/~kelseydb/Exhibits/AncientNubia/index.html

This University of Michigan site about an exhibit titled: "Ancient Nubia: Egypt's Rival in Africa" includes information and photos about the building of the first Aswan Dam and photos from the exhibit.

"The Nubia Salvage Project"
www-oi.uchicago.edu/OI/PROJ/NUB/Nubia.html

This site is by the Oriental Institute of Chicago. It describes an excavation project near the Aswan High Dam in Upper Egypt (Lower Nubia) in 1960–1964. The site also has information about the exhibit "Nubia: Its Glory and Its People," which was based on artifacts collected during the excavation.

Name _____

Date _____

Clues and Theories

- *Objective:* To think about how archaeologists find objects and study them, which leads to theories about how people lived in the past
- *Time to Complete Activity:* About an hour
- *Materials Needed:* Paper and pencil

- *Directions:* Read the following story.

You are walking in the woods one day. You find a dirt road. This road leads to an old house. The door is hanging open, windows are broken, and weeds and vines have grown up. It looks as if no one has lived in the house for a long time. You decide to look around, and you find a few things left by people who had been in the house.

In one of the closets you find a scrap of newspaper that has a date: July 11, 1947.

In what was the kitchen, you find a broken glass milk bottle.

In the middle of one of the rooms, you see some burned logs, matches, and an empty sardine can.

Out in the yard, you find a long length of chain hanging from a tree limb and a large oily stain on the ground beside the house. In the bushes is a rusted metal tricycle with one wheel missing.

To your surprise, you also find a grave behind the house. The grave is very small and has a wooden marker on it that says "Fluffy."

- Think about the **clues** you found in the house and yard. Put these clues together to form your own opinions or **theories** about people who had been in the house—how they lived and played; what they ate; whether they were young or old; etc.

- Jot down your ideas.

- Discuss and exchange ideas with the others in your group.

Wonders of World Cultures—Exploring Africa

SECTION I

Archaeological Wonders

(Clues and Theories)

CHAPTER 1: Nubia— Wonders in the Tumuli

Chapter Summary

What are the "wonders" in this story?

The wonders in this story are artifacts found in the burial tumuli (mounds) of Ballana and Qustol, in Lower Nubia, by Professor Walter B. Emery and his team in the early 1930's.

What are the major themes about Nubia and Nubian civilization covered in the story and activities in this chapter?

- Nubia and Egypt were the two great civilizations that developed along the Nile River.

- Meroë, in Upper Nubia, became the focus of the Nubian civilization from about 300 B.C. to A.D. 350.
- Building the Aswan Dam in the early 1930's threatened artifacts in Lower Nubia and prompted an archaeological survey of the area.
- The burial mounds (tumuli) of Lower Nubia that were excavated in the early 1930's by Walter B. Emery and his team yielded many archaeological treasures, but unanswered questions remain about the people who made the mounds.

Answer to "Think About It" Question

(page 5)

The Nile River flows from south to north, flowing into the Mediterranean Sea. In geographic names "upper" refers to an area that is closer to the source of a river, and "lower" refers to an area that is closer to the ending part of a river.

Answers to "Your Theory" Questions

(page 7)

Most natural hills are not as round in shape as the ones at Ballana and Qustol, which leads Emery to believe that the hills are not natural but artificial.

Emery's theory is that the ax heads, which were probably attached to ax handles originally, and the animals and men who cared for them were buried with the deceased person so that he would have use of them in the afterlife. In other words, the Nubians believed that they could take these things with them after death.

The arrangement of the objects in the entrance of the tomb, rather than in the tomb itself, suggests to Emery that the objects were gifts to the gods.

(page 8)

The Egyptian influences include the images of Egyptian gods and designs and the iron-making tools, an invention borrowed from the Egyptians. African influences include the leather shields used by African tribesmen. Roman influences include the Roman-type game box that was found in a tomb.

Answers to "Thought/Discussion" Questions _____

(page 11)

1. The dam provides a reliable supply of water for growing crops, for Egyptian homes and businesses, and for hydroelectric power (electricity generated from the energy of running water).

2. Answers will vary.

3. It is not known what happened to archaeological treasures that grave robbers stole in ancient times. Perhaps they melted the gold and silver for resale to whomever would buy it.

In the 1800's and early 1900's, museums, collectors, and tourists were eager to buy whatever ancient artifacts were available. Therefore, gangs of grave robbers scoured Egypt and Nubia to find treasures to sell.

Bibliography _____

Adult Books

Emery, Walter B. *Lost Land Emerging.* New York: Scribner's, 1967.

Haynes, Joyce L. *Nubia: Ancient Kingdoms of Africa.* Boston: Museum of Fine Arts, 1994.

Keating, Rex. *Nubian Twilight.* New York: Harcourt, Brace & World, 1963.

Shinnie, P.L. *Ancient Nubia.* London and New York: Kegan Paul International, 1996.

Juvenile Books

Bianchi, Robert. *The Nubians: People of the Ancient Nile.* Brookfield, CT: Millbrook Press, 1994.

Jenkins, Ernestine. *A Glorious Past: Ancient Egypt, Ethiopia, and Nubia.* New York: Chelsea House, 1995.

CHAPTER 1:
Nubia—Wonders in the Tumuli

Crown of an X-Group queen, decorated with carnelians (a red or reddish-brown stone)

AFRICA

① The focus of this chapter is Nubia, especially Lower Nubia, approximately 300 B.C.–A.D. 350.

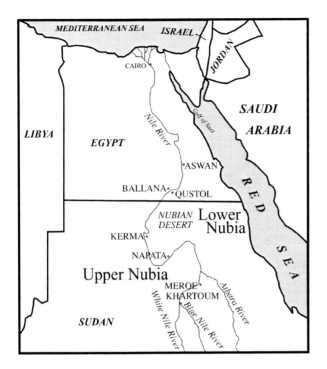

Think About It—

Why is Upper Nubia to the south of Lower Nubia? Also, in ancient times, Lower Egypt was near the northern end of the Nile and Upper Egypt was to the south. Can you explain this? (Hint: In what direction does the Nile River flow?)

Neighbors: Nubians and Egyptians

Archaeologists call the first Nubian people to trade with the Egyptians the **A-Group** of about 3800–3100 B.C.

From about 1500 B.C., Egypt occupied a large part of Nubia and collected taxes in the form of luxury goods—gold, ivory, ebony, ostrich feathers and eggs, wild animals, and incense. The pharoahs of Egypt became very wealthy.

When Egypt's central government weakened, a Nubian king conquered Egypt and became pharaoh in about 724 B.C. This Nubian pharaoh was named Piankhy (the "living one") and was the first of a series of Nubians who ruled Egypt for 60 years. Finally, a powerful Assyrian army conquered Egypt and pushed the Nubian kings back to their homeland.

The Wonders of Upper Nubia

Archaeologists discovered ruins of palaces, temples, and houses in the remains of Meroë, the capital of the kingdom of Meroë of Upper Nubia from about 300 B.C.–A.D. 350. The names of kings, queens, and gods were written in Egyptian hieroglyphic writing on the walls of the ruins. Beautiful pottery was found in Meroë. Some of the pottery, such as jars with a polished black surface, were made in Nubia. Some of the pottery had Egyptian, Greek, and Roman designs, which showed that it probably came from outside Nubia. (Egypt was conquered by Greece in 332 B.C. and by the Roman Empire in 31 B.C.)

The Two Great Civilizations of the Nile River

You probably know about the Egyptian civilization that grew up along the Nile River. No doubt you have heard of Egypt's mummies, pyramids, and hieroglyphic writing.

Do you also know about the other great civilization that developed along the Nile, but farther south—the **Nubian civilization**? (See map above.)

Both Egypt and Nubia were mostly desert and depended on the Nile River for survival. In ancient times, the only area fertile enough to grow food was a narrow strip of land along the banks of the Nile. Rich soil was washed onto this strip of land during the annual flood, and water from the river was available for crops.

Both civilizations had pyramids and a written language. The Egyptian hieroglyphic language was decoded in the 1800's. The Nubian language, which borrowed some hieroglyphs from the Egyptians, has never been completely decoded.

Nubians were (and are) black Africans. This Nubian prince is from a wall painting in the tomb of Huy, an Egyptian official of about 1334 B.C.

Aswan Dam to Flood Lower Nubia!

After the Egyptian government increased the height of the Aswan Dam on the Nile, areas of Lower Nubia would be flooded when the construction was finished, after 1912. This prompted the first archaeological surveys of Lower Nubia, from 1907 to 1911. More than 50 cemeteries, a fortress, and a Roman camp were explored. This archaeological exploration uncovered the general sequence of Nubian history.

In the early 1930's, the Egyptian government planned to enlarge the Aswan Dam again. More areas of Lower Nubia would be flooded, creating a huge reservoir, or artificial lake. Whatever treasures were hidden underground would be lost forever under the reservoir.

In 1929, Walter B. Emery, of the University of London, was hired to explore the ruins of Lower Nubia that would be covered by the new reservoir.

Join Emery and his team as they race to uncover the "wonders of the tumuli." In these ancient treasures the archaeologists find **clues** that lead to **theories** (opinions) about the Nubian people. You will get a chance to take on the role of archaeologist, too.

Emery and His Team in Lower Nubia

Because the temperature can rise to 120° F in Lower Nubia in the summer, Emery plans to explore and dig during the winter months of 1929 to 1931. During the first two winters, nothing of great scientific interest is found. In November 1931, Emery and his team begin their third season in Lower Nubia.

Clues in the Landscape at Ballana and Qustol

Imagine you are with Emery and his team of 150 workers as they explore the hot desert country near the Nile, looking for clues to the location of ruins of ancient towns or graves.

Emery comes upon what he thinks are hills covered with small, stunted trees. Climbing to the top of one of the hills, he can see that all the hills are very round. Other members of the group also remark that these hills seem too perfectly round.

Suddenly, the team is distracted by reports of grave robbers at Qustol, the other site that is to be explored.

At Qustol, the small hills are even more round in shape.

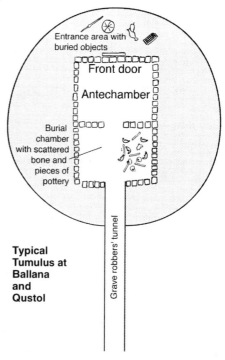

Entrance area with buried objects
Front door
Antechamber
Burial chamber with scattered bone and pieces of pottery
Grave robbers' tunnel

Typical Tumulus at Ballana and Qustol

Which to Dig First—Ballana or Qustol?

After looking at the mounds at Qustol, Emery sees that they all have a slight depression on one side. He scratches at one of the depressions and finds pieces of broken pottery, probably dropped by ancient grave robbers. This is probably the entrance to a robber's tunnel.

To save time, Emery decides to use the robber's tunnel to go into the largest mound at Qustol. (See map, previous page.) At the end of the tunnel is a room that he explores by candlelight. He is disappointed to see how completely the robbers did their job. All they left was broken pottery, moldy pieces of wood, and human bones scattered around.

In another room, which Emery calls the antechamber, the front door to the tomb is still shut and sealed with mud brick. Emery thinks there could be an area beyond the front door that may hold treasures the robbers did not find. He has another decision to make: Should he spend his limited time investigating the items the robbers left behind in the rooms, or should he explore the area in front of the door and risk finding nothing? What would you advise him to do?

Clues in the Mound Entrance

Emery decides to dig out the entrance area of another, smaller mound at Qustol. His decision is rewarded when the workers find two perfectly preserved ax heads in the sand in front of the entrance. Then they find skeletons of horses, donkeys, and camels all piled together, and also the skeletons of men. The horses' saddles are wooden and decorated with silver trim.

More Treasures in the Big Mound

Since the entrance area of one mound contained Nubian treasures, Emery thinks it is likely that all of the tumuli entrances contain treasures. The workers start digging out the entrance to the largest mound at Qustol—the same mound they have entered through the robber's tunnel.

Even with a 150-person crew, the digging goes slowly, but eventually objects are uncovered. They have been scattered throughout the sand of the entrance area "like currants [raisins] in a cake, or coins in a Christmas pudding," according to Emery.

Diggers find a large, circular leather shield, like those used by the Bega tribe of Nubia, knives, and the blade of a spear. The ivory handle of one of the knives is carved to look like the ancient Egyptian god Bes.

One of the most interesting things the workers find is a game board with a silver carrying handle. Five ivory dice marked 1 to 6 and a Roman-type box for shaking and throwing the dice are found with the board.

After finding more remains of animals and men in the outer room, the excavators find that the tomb itself has been thoroughly robbed. Only a tangled heap of human bones and broken pottery has been left behind.

The other tumuli at Qustol reveal similar offerings buried in the entrance areas, as well as sacrificed animals, including silver horse decorations, and remains of people.

Back to Ballana

Floodwaters from the Nile have welded the mud bricks of the Ballana tombs into a solid, rocklike mass. Objects have to be cut out, making the work much more difficult than at Qustol.

On the positive side, however, because robbers also found the work difficult, they left one tomb completely undisturbed.

In the burial chamber of this mound, Emery finds the skeleton of a Nubian king, still wearing his silver crown. He also wears necklaces and bracelets and silver archer's equipment with ancient Egyptian designs. His body was laid to rest on a wooden bed with a mattress made of woven rope. The bed had actually fallen apart over time, but impressions of it can still be seen on the floor.

Skeletons of a large dog, a camel, and three humans are found in the same room with the king. In another room is the skeleton of a female with a silver crown, perhaps the queen, and the bones of her sacrificed servants.

Two more rooms in the mound contain many items that the king would need in the afterlife. Bronze lamps, tables, incense burners, balances with a set of weights, and pottery jars that probably had food and drink in them. You see that gardening tools were provided to help prepare the soil to grow food in the next life.

You also find swords, spears, and iron-making tools to forge new weapons in the afterlife when the old ones wore out. This was a tradition borrowed from the Egyptians.

Emery's Summary

Even with all of the treasures recovered from the tumuli at Ballana and Qustol, Emery is disappointed about the knowledge he has gained about the X-Group people, as he calls them. He does not know where they came from.

✍ **Your Theory**

You agree with Emery that the items found in the tombs show a mix of influences: Egyptian, Roman, and African. What clues in the story lead you to this theory?

Clearly, much more work needs to be done in the area of research into this period of Nubian history. Unfortunately, the waters of the dammed-up Nile River have probably covered up most of the clues that would help archaeologists develop more theories about the Nubian civilization.

Name _____

Date _____

Nubian Pottery Decoration

The Nubians were well known for their beautiful pottery.

Archaeologists call one group of Nubians who lived from about 2000 to 1500 B.C. the **C-Group** people. They made polished black pottery with geometric designs etched onto the surface. These designs are often filled with white glaze and look like copies of basketry patterns. The C-Group people made their pottery by hand, rather than on a potter's wheel.

C-Group Pot

From about 300 B.C. to A.D. 350, the kingdom of Meroë was the focus of the Nubian people. They produced pottery using a wheel. To decorate the pottery, they painted designs of animals and plants.

Pot from Meroë

- ◆ *Objective:* To create a small "pinch pot" and decorate it with a Nubian design
- ◆ *Time to Complete Activity:* 1–2 hours
- ◆ *Materials Needed:* White modeling compound that can be hardened in an oven; toothpicks; felt-tip pens or water-based acrylic or tempera paints; small, finely tapered brush if using paint; smooth-sided drinking glass; oven

Directions:

___ Work a small amount of modeling compound in your hands until it is soft. Roll it into a ball and place it on a flat, hard surface.

___ Starting at the top, push down into the ball with both thumbs until they are within about $\frac{1}{4}$ inch of the bottom.

___ With thumb on the inside and other fingers on the outside, pinch the compound to form walls on the pot.

___ When the walls of the pot are about $\frac{1}{4}$ inch thick, roll a small, smooth glass gently along the outside of the pot while you hold and support the pot from the inside with your fingers. This is to smooth out the surface of the pot a little.

___ If you are creating an etched pattern, use a toothpick to etch or draw a shallow pattern on the outside of the pot like the drawing you see of the C-Group pottery on this page. Bake the pot in an oven at 275°F for 15 minutes.

___ If you are drawing a design like that from Meroë, first bake the pot in an oven at 275°F for 15 minutes. Let the pot cool, then use a felt-tip pen or paint to create designs of plants or animals.

A 1500-Year-Old Murder Mystery (Was It Really Murder?)

◆ *Objective:* To think about clues, then think of a theory based on those clues

◆ *Time to Complete Activity:* 1 hour

◆ *Materials Needed:* This sheet, extra paper, pencil or pen

Variation: Write a play set in Nubia based on the burials you read about, the grave robbers, and the girl.

Directions:

___ After reading the chapter "Nubia—Wonders in the Tumuli," read the following story of a very unusual discovery made by Emery and his team.

As Emery and his team of diggers worked in the hot, dry desert of Nubia, near the top of one of the mounds they discovered a bunch of brightly-colored cloth. Inside the cloth was the well-preserved body of a girl. She was preserved so well by the dry sand that Emery could see how she had died. There was a long cut on her throat, and there were brown blood stains on the cut and on her dress.

Beside the girl, Emery found two sacks, one made of linen and one of thick leather, both in poor condition. The sacks contained many valuable objects including small delicately carved wooden bottles, one in the form of an Egyptian sphinx and the other carved as the Egyptian god Ra. The bottles had originally held black eye make-up called kohl. The sacks also contained jewelry, including silver earrings set with precious stones, five silver rings, a silver and coral necklace, and a silver bracelet.

Near the girl was found a large, wooden chest decorated on the front panel with ivory and ebony designs. The lock had been cut off, and the chest was empty.

___ What is your theory about what happened to the girl? Write down your ideas on the lines at the right.

_____

_____

_____

_____

_____

_____

_____

_____

_____

_____

_____

_____

_____

_____

_____

Thought/Discussion Questions

1. The Aswan Dam was built and enlarged several times in order to help the growing population of Egypt. List the ways you think the dam could help Egypt.

_____

_____

_____

_____

2. When the Aswan Dam was built, and later when it was enlarged, there were protests from around the world that precious archaeological treasures would be covered by the waters of the reservoir created by the dam.

   Have you heard of any developers or builders who wanted to construct houses, industrial plants, or other structures that might cover up or destroy areas that contained archaeological treasures? Did they come into conflict with archaeologists and others who wanted to protect and excavate the area? What happened?

_____

_____

_____

_____

_____

_____

3. Most of the tumuli excavated by Emery and his team had been plundered by grave robbers. What do you think happened to the goods that were stolen?

_____

_____

_____

_____

CHAPTER 2: Great Zimbabwe— A Mystery and a Wonder

Chapter Summary

What is the "wonder" in this story?

The wonder in this story is Great Zimbabwe, the largest ancient stone ruins of southern Africa.

What are the major themes about Great Zimbabwe covered in this chapter?

- For centuries, foreign visitors to Africa refused to believe that the ancestors of native Africans had built Great Zimbabwe.

- Before professional archaeologists came to Great Zimbabwe, hunters, amateur archaeologists, writers, gold prospectors, and many other people damaged the ruins; this made it difficult for future excavators to compile correct information.

- Through the work of professional archaeologists and others, it was determined that ancestors of local native Africans had built and lived in Great Zimbabwe.

- It was also determined that Great Zimbabwe was built and occupied during the Middle Ages, approximately A.D. 1000–1500.

- After excavating the ruins and studying the artifacts found there, professional archaeologists have concluded that Great Zimbabwe was a religious and trading center.

Answers to "Think About It" Question

(page 15)   The pyramids of Egypt, especially the ones at Giza, are very large. The Great Pyramid at Giza is 485 feet tall and 756 feet on each side.

Answers to "Your Theory" Questions

(pages 17– 18)

Who built Great Zimbabwe?

It is very likely that the local people who were living near Great Zimbabwe when Randall-MacIver was there learned how to make bracelets, tools, weapons, and pottery from older family members. Since the things they were making were similar to things found at Great Zimbabwe, then the original people of the ruins were probably distant family members (ancestors) of the local people. These ancestors passed on their knowledge through the generations to the local people.

When was Great Zimbabwe built?

Because of the glass and china found there, Randall-MacIver thinks that trade with the world outside Africa was going on at Great Zimbabwe during the 1300's–1400's. He believes that the stone structures built at Great Zimbabwe were built during that time.

Why was Great Zimbabwe built?

The soapstone birds, monoliths, and small figures found at Great Zimbabwe point to the possibility that it was built as a religious center.

The simple, stylized designs of the birds and figures could mean they were symbols, and may have been used in rituals or ceremonies. The way the monoliths were grouped along walls or on platforms and their large numbers could mean they were also symbols. Like the Venda iron rods, they may have stood for ancestors. It seems likely that the people at Great Zimbabwe used these things in rituals of a religion that honored ancestors.

The foreign objects obviously came from overseas to a town on the coast of Africa. From there, they reached Great Zimbabwe in the interior. The glass beads were an item of trade between the coast and the interior of Africa. Therefore, Great Zimbabwe was probably a trading center. This could be one reason why more people lived there and grew rich enough to build great stone enclosures.

The ironwire, hoes, axes, and other items were probably local trading items. Not only was Great Zimbabwe trading foreign goods through coastal towns, but it was also trading local goods with different groups in the interior.

Answer to "The Geography of African Trade Routes"

(page 20)

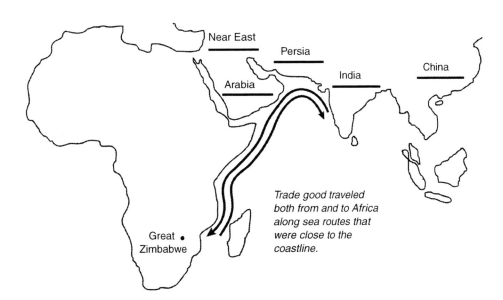

Answers to "Thought/Discussion" Questions

(page 21)   1–3. Answers will vary.

Bibliography

Adult Books

Garlake, P.S. *Great Zimbabwe.* New York: Stein and Day, 1973.

Huffman, Thomas N. *Symbols in Stone: Unraveling the Mystery of Great Zimbabwe.* Johannesburg: Witwatersrand University Press, 1987.

Mallows, Wilfrid. *The Mystery of the Great Zimbabwe: A New Solution.* New York: W.W. Norton, 1984.

Juvenile Books

Sheehan, Sean. *Zimbabwe.* New York: Marshall Cavendish, 1993.

Jacobsen, Karen. *Zimbabwe.* Chicago: Children's Press, 1990.

CHAPTER 2:
Great Zimbabwe—
A Mystery and a Wonder

Curved steps in an entrance
to the Great Enclosure at
Great Zimbabwe

AFRICA

②   The focus of this chapter is the ruins of Great Zimbabwe, A.D. 1000–1500.

Southern Africa

Labels on map: Democratic Republic of Congo, Tanzania, Angola, Zambia, Mozambique, Zimbabwe, Namibia, Botswana, Madagascar, Ruins of Great Zimbabwe, Swaziland, Lesotho, South Africa

> **Think About It—**
>
> *Great Zimbabwe has the largest ancient structure in southern Africa. What are the largest ancient stone structures in northern Africa?*

Great Stone Walls

Great Zimbabwe's stacked granite walls, mysterious cone-shaped tower, and stone columns pointing toward the sky are all treasures of African culture.

Zimbabwe Hill has a cliff on one side. The top of the hill is strewn with enormous boulders. A maze of ruined walls connects the boulders to form pockets, or enclosures. The largest is called the Western Enclosure. It has curved walls more than 30 feet high, as tall as a modern three-story building. Large columns of carved stone with carved birds on top were found inside this enclosure.

Zimbabwe Hill overlooks a valley. On the opposite side of the valley stands the greatest structure of Great Zimbabwe. Once it was known to local people as "the house of the great woman." Now it is called the Great Enclosure, or the Elliptical Building, because its outer wall forms a huge rough ellipse (flattened circle). This wall is the largest ancient structure in southern Africa. It is more than 800 feet long and at its largest point, 17 feet thick and 32 feet high. One of the most interesting things is that the wall starts out being about 15 feet high and poorly constructed. As it curves around, it gets higher and the construction gets better. Along its most carefully built section, granite blocks of the same size and shape are stacked in neat rows without mortar to hold them together. Each row of stones is set back a little, so the whole wall slopes back.

A solid circular tower, called the Conical Tower, stands inside the Great Enclosure. The tower is 18 feet across and 30 feet high and made of beautiful stonework.

In the valley between the Great Enclosure and Zimbabwe Hill are a series of small enclosures.

Who built these great structures? When and why did they build them? Answers to these questions eventually provided a treasure of knowledge about the African people, but early explorers in the region refused to believe that Africans could have built Great Zimbabwe. For centuries, foreign visitors invented fantastic (and untrue) stories to try to explain Great Zimbabwe.

Tall Tales

The first report about Great Zimbabwe came from a Portuguese writer named João de Barros, who probably got his information from African traders. In 1552, he wrote about a fortress built of huge stones without mortar between them, a very long wall, and a tower. He said the local people called these buildings *symbaoe,* but they didn't know who built them.

The local people (the Karanga) could not provide any information about the ruins, so the Portuguese made up their own stories about who built them.

They believed that the Bible was the most accurate source of information about the past. They also wanted to believe old stories that somewhere in Africa were great riches of gold. The gold-filled land of Ophir mentioned in the Bible, they believed, was probably Zimbabwe. They also believed that King Solomon of Israel had sent his navy there to find gold and supposedly built Great Zimbabwe. People believed these stories for centuries.

In 1868, Carl Mauch, a German geologist, not an archaeologist, was the first to explore the ruins in person and write reports about what he saw. He said that the local Karanga people did not know who built the structures, and, like the Portuguese, he made up his own stories. He claimed that the Queen of Sheba, who had visited King Solomon, was actually the one who had built "the house of the great woman" (the Great Enclosure).

These stories became very widespread. When people heard the name Great Zimbabwe, they thought of foreign kings, queens, and gold—but not of the local Africans.

In 1891, J. Theodore Bent, of Britain, found household objects like pieces of pottery, arrowheads, axes, and gardening tools that were very similar to ones that local people were still using. But he still looked to foreigners as builders of the structures at Great Zimbabwe. Bent decided people from Arabia who were related to the Egyptians had built the ruins.

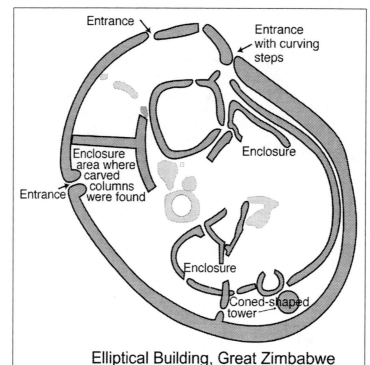

Elliptical Building, Great Zimbabwe

This is an overhead view of the largest structure at Great Zimbabwe. It is called a "building," but it is made of walls only and has no roof. All of the walls are made of stacked stone.

The Ruins Are Damaged

In the late 1800's, white settlers from South Africa came to the area that became the country of Rhodesia (later the country of Zimbabwe). Prospectors dug into almost all the ruins in the area looking for the gold that they had heard about. Not much gold was found, but many of the ruins were damaged.

Cecil Rhodes, a businessman and leader in southern Africa, came under pressure by the public to do something about the destruction of ruins in Rhodesia. In 1902, he hired Richard Hall, a writer, to investigate the ruins at Great Zimbabwe.

Hall did not have any experience investigating ruins. He and his team cleared away all the trees and vines from the stone structures, then they dug up and removed 5 to 12 feet of dirt and objects from inside the walls. They removed objects without recording the layers of rock and dirt they were found in. This made it very difficult to tell which time period they came from. For instance, if an object came from the lowest layer, it probably would have been among the oldest objects. In his writings about the site, Hall agreed with tall tales that said the original builders of Great Zimbabwe came from Arabia and the Middle East.

Wanted: Experienced Archaeologists

Finally, people who were interested in African history began to realize that experienced archaeologists were needed to excavate Great Zimbabwe.

David Randall-MacIver, an archaeologist who had worked in Egypt, was chosen to be the first professional excavator.

Follow along as Randall-MacIver and another archaeologist investigate Great Zimbabwe at the beginning of the 1900's. You will read about the clues they discovered and the theories they thought of to answer the questions: Who built Great Zimbabwe? When was it built?

You will get a chance to take on the role of archaeologist and think of theories, too.

Randall-MacIver

Who built Great Zimbabwe?

Imagine you are with Randall-MacIver and his team as they investigate the ruins.

Clues: *Daga,* made of clay mixed with small gravel, is the building material that Africans used, and still use, to make huts and floors. Randall-MacIver digs down through the thick daga floor of the Great Enclosure in eight places and finds coils of copper wire for making bracelets, tools, weapons, and pottery. These objects are very similar to the ones made by the native Africans who live nearby.

> ✎ **Your Theory**
>
> From the clues found, whom do you think built Great Zimbabwe?

When was Great Zimbabwe built?

Clues: Randall-MacIver says that the decorations on the pottery and the shapes of the tools and weapons are very simple and easily made. He also remembers that Hall found what he called "Arabian glass" and "Nankin china."

Since the pottery design and the tools are so simple, according to Randall-MacIver, they could have been made anywhere at any time, even by modern peoples. Therefore, he says, he cannot use them to decide when Great Zimbabwe was built or occupied.

On the other hand, he thinks the glass is like that made in Arabia in the fourteenth century and proba-

bly came to Zimbabwe through trade. Likewise, he thinks the china that Hall found was made in China in the fifteenth century. He believes Great Zimbabwe dates from about that time.

> ✎ **Your Theory**
>
> From the clues found by Randall-MacIver, when do you think Great Zimbabwe was built?

Gertrude Caton-Thompson

In 1929, the well-known archaeologist Gertrude Caton-Thompson excavates the ruins at Great Zimbabwe. Like Randall-MacIver before her, Caton-Thompson began her career in Egypt.

After digging out the entire area inside one of the ruins, she finds the same kinds of objects Randall-MacIver found. She agrees with him that ancestors of local people were the ones who built the ruins.

This is one of the entrances to the Elliptical Building. These steps curve into a walkway that is only wide enough for one person.

She does not find any objects in the ruins that came from outside Africa, so she is not sure if she can agree with Randall-MacIver that Great Zimbabwe dates from the fourteenth to fifteenth century.

When was Great Zimbabwe built?

Clues: Determined to find some evidence of when Zimbabwe was built, Caton-Thompson digs in a rubbish heap outside the Western Enclosure on Zimbabwe Hill.

At last, she finds objects that came from outside Africa. In the dump are a hundred tiny cylinder-shaped glass beads in black, white, yellow, red, and blue. They look like they were made in a simple process—broken off from a tube of glass and reheated to smooth the edges of each tiny bead.

Caton-Thompson asks an expert where the beads might have come from and when. Unfortunately, he cannot give a date for them. They are so simply made they could have been made yesterday or centuries ago. The mystery of when Great Zimbabwe was built is still not completely solved.

Modern Scientific Testing Helps Date Great Zimbabwe

In the early 1950's, radiocarbon dating was invented. Every living organism contains radiocarbon (carbon 14). By testing how much radiocarbon is left in a fossil, such as a bone, a piece of coal, or piece of wood, the age of the object can be determined.

Testing pieces of charcoal in several areas of the ruins at Great Zimbabwe gave dates ranging from about A.D. 1075 to 1440.

Why Was It Built?—You Decide

Today, it is possible to visit Great Zimbabwe as a tourist. You can climb Zimbabwe Hill along a modern path or use one of the ancient paths. A museum, a gift shop, and several hotels are nearby. The guidebook that is sold to tourists says that "the precise origin of this cultural complex is still debated by archaeologists and historians." In other words, it is still not known for sure what caused the native peoples to build Great Zimbabwe.

✎ **Your Theory**

After reading the following list of objects found at Great Zimbabwe and the information about local cultures, try to come up with your own theories about why the structures were built and why the people were prosperous enough to build such an elaborate village.

Eight carved soapstone birds were found at Great Zimbabwe and nowhere else. They were removed from their original places in the ruins, so it's impossible to know if they were originally inside the walls or mounted on the walls. All the birds are about 14 inches high. They are attached to the top of columns 3 feet high. The carvings do not look like real birds. For instance, the feet have toes rather than talons, and the wings are stiff and solid.

Columns, or *monoliths*, without birds were found in many areas of Great Zimbabwe. They were put in rows along the tops of the main outer walls, or in groups on low platforms, towers, and what look like altars. The local Venda people use iron rods to stand for and honor their ancestors—this might be a clue to the purpose of the columns at Zimbabwe.

Small figures of cattle and sheep were also found at Great Zimbabwe. They are not realistic figures of animals, but simplified with few details.

A small painted Persian bowl, made in the thirteenth or fourteenth century, pale-green Chinese dishes, engraved glass from the Near East, at least 20,000 beads, and many other objects were found by Hall in a ruin near the Great Enclosure.

A huge amount of iron wire, many hoes for farming, axes, chisels, copper, ivory, spearheads, iron gongs, and three iron rods used to ring the gongs were also found by Hall.

Soapstone birds were carved on top of columns from soft stone of a dark green-gray color.

Name _____

Date _____

Making a Copper Bracelet

In the Middle Ages, the people of Great Zimbabwe, in what is now the country of Zimbabwe, built large, mysterious stone-walled enclosures. These are the largest ancient stone structures in southern Africa.

In the ruins of Great Zimbabwe were found copper and iron wire. People used them to make decorative bangles to wear around the wrists, forearms, ankles, and calves. The remains of one female excavated in a ruin near Great Zimbabwe had more than $4\frac{1}{2}$ pounds of wire on each leg. The local Venda people wear similar ornaments today.

- ◆ *Objective:* To make a copper wire bracelet
- ◆ *Time to Complete Activity:* 2–3 hours
- ◆ *Materials Needed:* Medium-weight cardboard (a paper egg carton works well), masking tape, a 50-foot roll of 20-gauge copper wire, wire cutters, scissors

---

Directions:

— Cut a piece of the cardboard 10 inches long and 1 inch wide.

— Fold the cardboard in half lengthwise.

— Wrap masking tape tightly around and around the cardboard strip, leaving about 1 inch from one end of cardboard free of tape. Repeat so you have two layers of masking tape. This is your base to wrap the wire around.

— Bend cardboard strip gently into a curved shape, but do not close it yet.

— Starting about 1 inch from one end of the strip, wrap copper wire around and around the strip, covering as much of the cardboard as possible.

— When you are 1 inch from the other end of the strip, stop wrapping the wire and cut it with a wire cutter.

— Insert the end of the strip with masking tape into the end without the tape. Because you folded the cardboard over, there will be an opening into which you can insert the end with the masking tape.

— Pull off about 10 feet of wire and roll it into a loose ball.

— Using the ball of wire, wind the copper wire around the remaining part of the bangle that doesn't have wire on it.

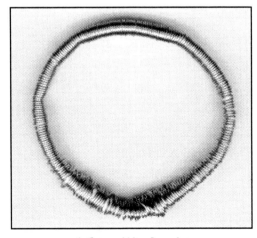

A Copper Wire Bracelet

The Geography of African Trade Routes

In the Middle Ages the people of Great Zimbabwe, in what is now the country of Zimbabwe, built large, mysterious stone-walled enclosures. These are the largest ancient stone structures in southern Africa.

Many pieces of objects that came from outside Africa have been found at Great Zimbabwe, which is a sign that it was a major trading center. Luxury items, like porcelain dishes from foreign lands, came to the eastern coast of Africa and were carried inland to Great Zimbabwe. There people traded their gold, ivory, iron, and cloth for the foreign luxury items.

◆ *Objective:* To become aware of the trade routes to the eastern coast of Africa

◆ *Time to Complete Activity:* 1 hour

◆ *Materials Needed:* World atlas, this page, pencil or pen

Directions:

On this page you see an outline of Africa and other areas of the world from which traders came to Africa. Below is a list of some of the foreign goods that came to the east coast of Africa and then were carried inland to Great Zimbabwe.

On the map, write the names of the countries or areas listed below. Also, write in the names of the oceans and draw possible sea trade routes.

Goods that came to Africa and were found at Great Zimbabwe and nearby sites:

• Persian bowls
• Chinese blue-and-white ceramic dishes
• Glass from the Near East
• Arabian glassware
• Beads from India

Outline map of Africa and trading areas

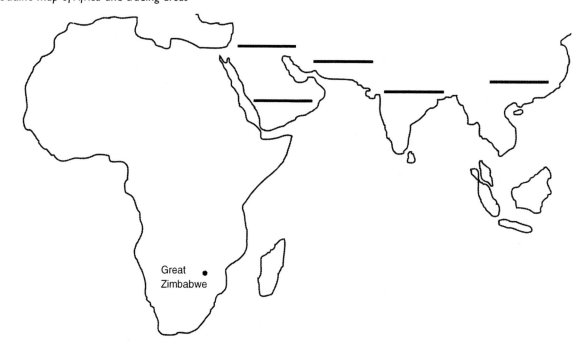

Name _____

Date _____

Thought/Discussion Questions

1. For centuries, people believed that Great Zimbabwe was a land of gold and that people from outside Africa, including King Solomon of Israel, had built the great stone walls. Why do you think people believed these stories even when there was evidence that they weren't true?

   _____

   _____

   _____

   _____

2. Do you think it's important for professional archaeologists to excavate ruins? Why or why not?

   _____

   _____

   _____

   _____

3. The Africans who built Great Zimbabwe used local materials to build the great stone walls and buildings in which they lived. Daga, which is clay mixed with small gravel, was used to build small houses, and floors inside the enclosures. Blocks of granite to build the walls of the enclosures came from bare, rounded hills of granite nearby. The top layers of the granite hills split off and slid to the bottom, so builders could collect them easily.

   What did the people who lived in your area originally use as building materials? What about the Europeans, Africans, and Asians who came later—what materials did they use to build their houses and walls?

   _____

   _____

   _____

   _____

   _____

SECTION 2

Other Treasures and Wonders of African Cultures

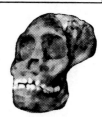

CHAPTER 3: *Fossil Wonders of Africa*

Chapter Summary

What are the "wonders" in this story?

The bones and stone tools of early humans found in southern and eastern Africa.

What are the major themes about the fossil record of early humans in Africa covered in the story and activities in this chapter?

- Humans are descended from apes.

- Humans did not evolve in a straight line from primitive types to more modern types. There were many branches to the human tree. One to three million years ago, apelike hominids lived at the same time as more modern hominids.

- Some of the traits associated with modern humans are larger brains, walking upright on two legs, smaller teeth, and smaller brow ridges.

Answers to "Charting Human Development"

(page 32)

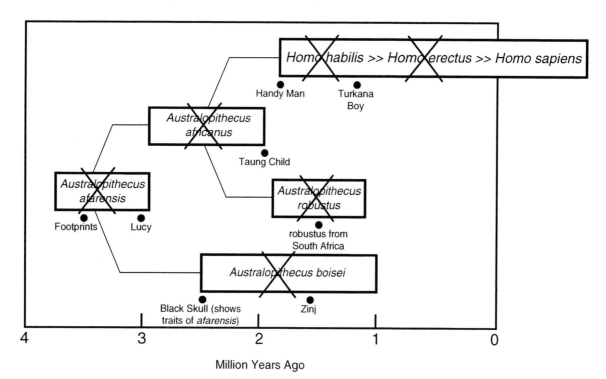

Million Years Ago

24

(page 33)

When was it alive?	What was found?	Where was it found?	Who found it?	When was it found?
c. 18 million years ago	Proconsul: - bridge between monkeys and apes - ancestor of gorilla, chimp, orangutan	Rusinga Island, Lake Victoria Rusinga	Leakey team Alan Walker	1948 1980's
c. 4 million years ago	Kanapoi Hominid: - chin/jawbone more apelike than Lucy - teeth more humanlike - could be new "missing link"	Kanapoi, Lake Turkana	Meave Leakey	1994
c. 3.5 million years ago	Fossilized hominid footprints: - made by hominids with feet similar to modern humans - oldest evidence of hominids walking upright	Laetoli	Mary/ Richard Leakey	1972
c. 3 million years ago	Lucy and First Family: - 3½ foot female - 13 other individuals - mix of ape and human traits - root stock of all hominids, Johanson said at the time	Hadar, Ethiopia	D. Johanson	1974
c. 2.6 million years ago	Black Skull: - blue-black in color - mix of *A. afarensis* (Lucy) and *A. boisei* (Zinj) traits	Koobi Fora, Lake Turkana	Leakey team	1985
c. 2 million years ago	Taung Child: *(Australopithecus africanus)* - "manlike ape" - walked upright *Australopithecus robustus:* - larger, stronger version of *A. africanus*	South Africa	Raymond Dart	1924
c. 1.8 million years ago	Handy Man: - larger brain than *(A. boisei)* Zinj - thinner bones than Zinj - named *Homo habilis* - modern humans evolved from Handy Man	Olduvai Gorge	Leakey team	1960
c. 1.75 million years ago	Zinj or Nutcracker Man: - small brain - huge jaws/powerful teeth - probably made simple pebble tools	Olduvai Gorge	Leakey team	1951
c. 1.54 million years ago	Turkana Boy: - brain smaller than modern humans - jaws and teeth larger than modern humans but not as large as *Australopithecus* - called *Homo erectus*	Lake Turkana	Leakey team	1984

Answer to "Think About It" Question _____

(page 31)

A scientist who studies human origins is called an anthropologist.

Answers to "Thought/Discussion" Questions _____

(page 35)

1. Answers will vary.

2. Answers will vary. (Scientists have theorized that bipedalism and larger brain size were adaptations to a changing, cooler climate about 5–7 million years ago.)

Bibliography _____

Adult Books

Johanson, Donald, Lenora Johanson, and Edgar Blake. *Ancestors: In Search of Human Origins.* New York: Villard Books, 1994.

Leakey, Richard. *The Origin of Humankind.* New York: Basic Books, 1994.

Lewin, Roger. *In the Age of Mankind: A Smithsonian Book of Human Evolution.* Washington, DC: Smithsonian Books, 1988.

Lewin, Roger. *Human Evolution: An Illustrated Introduction.* Boston: Blackwell Scientific Publications, 1989.

Morrell, Virginia. *Ancestral Passions.* New York: Simon & Schuster, 1995.

Readings from Scientific American: Human Ancestors. San Francisco: W.H. Freeman, 1979.

Juvenile Books

Heiligman, Deborah. *Mary Leakey: In Search of Human Beginnings.* New York: Freeman, 1995.

Willis, Delta. *The Leakey Family: Leaders in the Search for Human Origins.* New York: Facts on File, 1992.

Magazine Articles

Leakey, Meave. "The Dawn of Humans: The Farthest Horizon." *National Geographic,* Vol. 188, No. 3 (September 1995), pp. 38–51.

Johanson, Donald C. "The Dawn of Humans: Face-to-Face with Lucy's Family." *National Geographic,* Vol. 189, No. 3 (March 1996), pp. 96–117.

Gore, Rick. "The Dawn of Humans: Expanding Worlds." *National Geographic,* Vol. 191, No. 5 (May 1997), pp. 84–109.

CHAPTER 3:
Fossil Wonders of Africa

Many of the fossils found in Africa were preserved by the alkaline materials spewed out by volcanoes. Much later, volcanic and earthquake activity shifted the earth and exposed fossils that are millions of years old. Scientists cannot date fossils directly, so they test and read the dates of the levels of volcanic material above and below the fossils to get a rough idea of how old they are.

AFRICA

③ *The focus of this chapter is the fossil record of early humans in southern and eastern Africa from approximately 1 million to 18 million years ago.*

Map of Southern and Eastern Africa Showing Sites in Text

The Missing Link

What is the birthplace of humans? In other words, where did apes first evolve into early humans?

What is the "missing link" between apes and humans—the animal that first split off from apes to eventually become human?

The wealth of fossil bones and stone tools found in southern and eastern Africa leads many scientists to believe that Africa is the birthplace of humans and the source of the "missing link."

Taung Child

In 1924, Raymond Dart of South Africa was digging through some limestone from a quarry. He found part of the skull of a child who was about six

years old at the time of death. Dart was an anatomist—a person who knows a lot about bones and how the parts of the human body fit together. He looked at the place in the skull where the spinal column would have fit and decided that the child had walked more or less upright on two legs. Also, he thought the child's teeth were more human than ape, because the pointy canine teeth were not as large as those in apes.

Dart concluded that his find was a "manlike ape" and named it *Australopithecus africanus,* which means "southern ape from Africa." The child lived about 2 million years ago.

In the 1930's and 1940's, other scientists found skulls of more "manlike apes" in southern Africa. They were similar to *africanus* but had larger, heavier teeth and jaws and thicker ridges on their skulls for attaching strong muscles. These heavy-duty teeth and muscles were for chewing the tough plants they ate. This creature was named *Australopithecus robustus* (robust means strong and hardy).

Proconsul

In 1948, the husband and wife team of Louis and Mary Leakey were exploring Rusinga Island, which is near the eastern shore of Lake Victoria.

While wandering near the campsite, Mary found a tooth and several pieces of a skull. After shouting for Louis to come over, she started brushing away the dirt and found that the tooth was still in a jawbone. After digging for days and carefully putting together the pieces they found, the team saw that they had more than half of the skull of a creature they called *Proconsul,* which was alive about 18 million years ago.

More than 30 years after the Leakeys' discovery, scientists taking a new look at the *Proconsul* skull saw it had been pressed down on one side because it had been buried for millions of years. *Proconsul* had a larger skull and a larger brain than anyone had thought.

In the 1980's, a team of scientists led by Alan Walker went back to Rusinga Island and located the same hollowed-out spot that the Leakeys had dug in 1948. On the first day Walker and the team found so many fossils they couldn't carry them all. Using a bone here and a bone there, they were able to put together a partial skeleton of *Proconsul*.

This creature had some monkey and some apelike features. The larger brain, shoulder bones, and elbow bones point to apes. The long backbone, the arm, and the wrist bones are more monkeylike.

These remains have shown that *Proconsul* was a bridge between monkeys and apes. It was an ancestor of chimpanzees, gorillas, and orangutans—and millions of years later, of humans.

Zinj (also called Nutcracker Man)

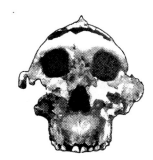

Olduvai Gorge is a 25-mile-long canyon in east Africa that lies between an extinct volcanic crater and the Serengeti National Park.

The Leakeys had been to Olduvai many times before, but in 1951 they went back to explore the area in depth. Their work was rewarded when they found thousands of stone tools and bones of many mammals, including an extinct animal that had giant hooves and horns 6 feet across. Bones of a pig as large as a hippo and a baboon the size of a gorilla were also found.

But they did not find bones of hominids (early humans) until much later, in 1959. Again, while walking around looking carefully at the ground for anything unusual, Mary noticed that recent rains had uncovered a small bone that was sticking up. After brushing away the dirt, she found parts of two large teeth still in a jawbone. Louis was called to the scene, and the team spent 19 days uncovering the skull, which was in 400 pieces.

Mary was very good at fitting pieces of bone together. The skull that she reconstructed was small, showing that the brain had also been small. The skull

had a ridge across the top. Large, powerful chewing muscles had been attached to the ridge, just like they were in gorillas. So, like gorillas, this hominid spent a lot of time chewing its food.

Nearby, the team found many simple pebble tools, which were made by sharpening one edge of a pebble. Animal bones found around the skull showed that the hominid had probably used the stone tools to cut meat from bones. The evidence showed that it ate both plants and meat.

This hominid was like the *Australopithecus robustus* found in South Africa. But Louis Leakey did not think that *robustus* had been a tool-user. Therefore, he thought he had a new hominid and named the skull *Zinjanthropus boisei*, nicknamed "Zinj." (*Zinjanthropus* means "East African Man.") It was also called Nutcracker Man because of its huge jaws and powerful teeth.

When other scientists recognized that the jaws and teeth were like those found in the *robustus* skulls in southern Africa, they renamed Nutcracker Man *Australopithecus boisei*, showing that he was a type of *Australopithecus*.

In articles and interviews, Louis Leakey claimed that his team had discovered the oldest hominid yet found and that Africa was the birthplace of humans. Testing the dates of volcanic levels above and below the bones proved that Leakey was right—the skull was 1.75 million years old, the oldest hominid skull found up to that time.

Handy Man

At Olduvai, in the summer of 1960, the Leakeys' oldest son, Jonathan, made another astounding discovery. First he found a leg bone, then others in the team found foot, toe, jaw, and skull bones. These bones were very different from those of Zinj. His were thick and heavy, but this new hominid's were thinner. Also, the new skull did not have the huge brow ridges, the thick ridge across the top of the skull, or the heavy grinding teeth of Zinj. Most important, the new hominid had a much larger brain.

Louis named this find *Homo habilis,* which means "handy man." He thought this was the only hominid at Olduvai that made and used tools.

The new find was about 1.8 million years old, putting it in the same range as *Australopithecus.* Louis claimed that modern humans had evolved from this new hominid, rather than from *Australopithecus.* He believed that Zinj and all others of the *Australopithecus* group had become extinct.

Lucy and the First Family

In 1974, a team of scientists led by Donald Johanson went to the scorching hot Hadar, in northern Ethiopia, where a large lake had been in ancient times. They found a huge number of hominid fossils, including a large portion of the skeleton of a 3½-foot female they nicknamed "Lucy," and parts of 13 other individuals they called "the first family."

These are the only skull bones of Lucy that were found.

Lucy and the others are 3 million years old—much older than the bones found at Olduvai. They have an odd mix of ape and human features. Apelike traits include small skulls, which means they had small brains. Their jawbones jutted out like those of apes, and they had long, apelike arms. The females were much smaller than the males, which is like those ape societies in which the males have to fight for the right to mate with females. Only the biggest and strongest males win these battles and get to mate.

Like humans, however, Lucy and the others walked upright, as shown by their pelvic and leg bones.

Johanson believed he had found the root stock from which all later hominids had come. He named Lucy and the others from Hadar *Australopithecus afarensis.*

Fossil Footprints

Louis Leakey died in 1972, but Mary Leakey and her son Richard have kept up the family tradition of fossil hunting.

In 1978, Mary and her team were in Laetoli, which is near Olduvai Gorge. While playing with dried elephant dung (which is like cakes of dried grass), one of Mary Leakey's friends fell down and found himself face to face with footprints of animals in hardened volcanic ash.

After two seasons of digging, footprints of three hominids were found in the same area. These hominids had feet similar in shape to modern humans.

Three and a half million years ago, a nearby volcano had spewed volcanic ash over the area. Then animals walked across the ash, a little rain fell, and the sun came out, baking the footprints as hard as cement. More ash fell, more animals walked across the area, rain fell again, and the sun came out, preserving a two-week record of activity. Even twigs, birds' eggs, beetles, and animal droppings were preserved in the ash.

Mary Leakey believed the largest hominid prints belonged to a male, the medium size ones to a female, and the smallest prints to a child. The child apparently walked behind and inside the male's footprints, like a child or a young ape playing follow the leader.

No stone tools were found in the area, so Leakey believed the footprints were made by hominids who walked upright before they used tools. This is the oldest evidence of human ancestors who walked upright.

Turkana Boy

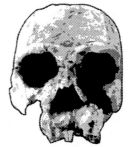

Lake Turkana is in northern Kenya on the border with Ethiopia. Not far from the lake is a desert where the temperatures are higher than 100 degrees all year long.

Near Lake Turkana, in 1984, one of Richard Leakey's associates, Kamoya Kimeu, discovered the almost-complete skeleton of a 12-year-old boy. It took four long seasons and the removal of 1,000 tons of soil for the team to finally dig up most of the boy's bones.

Tests showed he died about 1.54 million years ago. He had larger jaws and teeth than modern humans but not as large or strong as *Australopithecus*. He and others of his type are called *Homo erectus*.

He had a thick bony ridge under his eyebrows, and his brain was smaller than modern human's. He would not have been able to do any complex thinking (like math problems).

The boy's spine had a much smaller hole through which the spinal cord passed than modern human spines do. This means he did not have as many nerves going to the throat and lung areas and could not have controlled his breathing to speak in sentences as modern humans do.

The Black Skull

Just one year later, in 1985, another Leakey team member, Alan Walker, was walking around the Koobi Fora area on the shore of Lake Turkana. He noticed a piece of hominid skull. It was an unusual blue-black color. He called his wife to the site and the two got down on their hands and knees and carefully dug out enough of the black pieces to fit together the top part of a skull.

Richard Leakey rushed to the site and supervised the complete restoration of the "black skull," which is about 2.6 million years old. The skull is an odd mix of traits—in the back it is shaped like Johanson's 3-million-year-old Lucy *(afarensis)*, but the flat face, huge grinding teeth, and small brain are like that of the apelike Zinj *(boisei)*, dating from only 2 million years ago.

Summary

Scientists have decided that there is no simple straight line of evolution from Lucy *(afarensis)* to modern humans *(Homo sapiens)*. It seems that from 1 to 3 million years ago, many different kinds of hominids, some primitive and apelike and some more modern, lived at the same time in Africa. Perhaps they even lived next door to one another.

To get back to the questions at the beginning of this chapter: Yes, it would seem that Africa is the birthplace of humans, because of all the bones and tools of early humans that have been found there.

Until recently, Lucy *(Australopithecus afarensis)* seemed to be the "missing link"—the oldest hominid yet found that shows both apelike and human traits. In 1994, however, Meave Leakey (Richard Leakey's wife) and her team found 4-million-year-old jawbones at Kanapoi, which is also near Lake Turkana. The slope of the chin in the new jawbone was greater (more apelike) than Lucy's. However, the teeth in the new jawbones were more humanlike. Leakey believes she has found a new type of hominid that came before Lucy—perhaps the new "missing link."

More and more fossils are found every year, but there is still a huge span of time for which there are no fossil records—plenty of opportunity for young fossil hunters.

Think About It—

Scientists who study the origin of humans—the way our bodies, society, and behavior developed—are called by what name?

Name _____

Date _____

Charting Early Human Development

- ◆ *Objective:* To get a better idea of when early humans lived
- ◆ *Time to Complete Activity:* 1 hour
- ◆ *Materials Needed:* This page, pencil, dictionary or encyclopedia, and Chapter 3

Directions:

— Referring to the information in the chapter, fill in the chart on the next page. The first section has been completed as an example.

— The chart below shows one of the theories of early human development. The boxes show the period of time when each type of hominid lived. For instance, *Australopithecus boisei* lived about 1 to 2.5 million years ago (see the numbers at the bottom of the chart). Mark on this chart the fossils that are mentioned in the chapter (one of them has already been marked on the chart).

— Put an *X* on the names of extinct hominids.

— Write the name of modern humans at the end of the *Homo* box.

The Human Tree

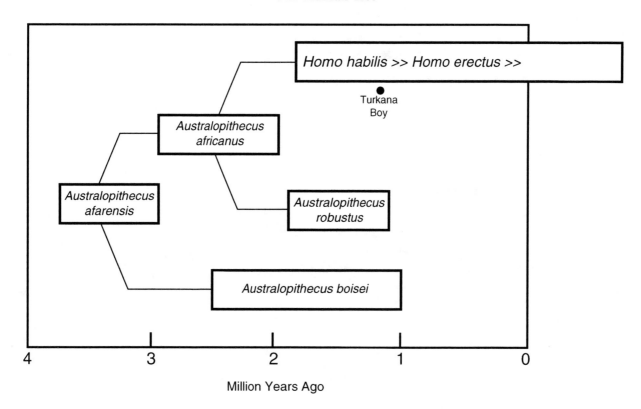

© 1998 J. Weston Walch, Publisher

32

Wonders of World Cultures—Exploring Africa

(continued)

Name _____

Date _____

Charting Early Human Development *(continued)*

When was it alive?	What was found?	Where was it found?	Who found it?	When was it found?
c. 18 million years ago	Proconsul: - bridge between monkeys and apes - ancestor of gorilla, chimp, orangutan	Rusinga Island, Lake Victoria	Leakey team Alan Walker	1948 1980's
	Kanapoi Hominid:			
	Fossilized hominid footprints:			
	Lucy and First Family:			
	Black Skull:			
	Taung Child: *(Australopithecus africanus)* *Australopithecus robustus:*			
	Handy Man: - named *Homo habilis*			
	Zinj or Nutcracker Man:			
	Turkana Boy:			

Name _____

Date _____

Identifying Bones

- ◆ *Objective:* To experience identifying bones
- ◆ *Time to Complete Activity:* 1 hour—over several days
- ◆ *Materials Needed:* Animal bones, index cards, felt-tip pens, small labeling dots, reference books, especially anatomy books

Directions:

— Collect as many bones of different animals as you can (washed and dried chicken bones, pork bones, beef bones could be brought from home).

— Number each bone with a labeling dot.

— Number the index cards and write the name of the animal and name of bone on the reverse side of the cards.

— Display the numbered bones and corresponding index cards so other students can try to identify the bones before they turn over the cards to see the answers.

Variation: Save the bones from a whole chicken, being careful not to break the bones. Clean and dry the bones. Place the bones on a table in their correct arrangement. Find and copy a picture of a chicken skull and place it where the skull bones should be.

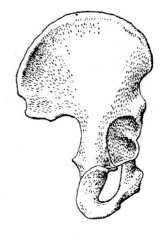

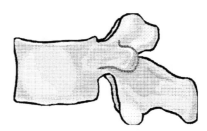

Do you know what part of the human body these bones come from? Answer is below.

(Illustrations by Techpool Studios, Inc.)

The one on top is a hipbone; the one on the bottom is a vertebra (section of the backbone).

Thought/Discussion Questions

1. Why do you think people search for the bones and tools of early humans?

_____

_____

_____

_____

_____

2. Bipedalism (walking on two legs) and a larger brain are the two main differences between humans and apes. Why do you think early humans developed these traits?

_____

_____

_____

_____

_____

_____

CHAPTER 4: *Rock Art Wonders of the Bushmen*

Chapter Summary

What is the "wonder" in this story?

The rock art of the Bushmen (San) of southern Africa

What are the major themes about the Bushmen and their art covered in this chapter?

- For thousands of years, the Bushmen of southern Africa created paintings and engravings (petroglyphs) that reflect their activities and beliefs.

Much of the artwork is still open to interpretation.

- Bushmen artists mastered rock painting and engraving techniques to create sensitive and detailed works of art.

- The arrival of Europeans into southern Africa threatened the Bushmen way of life and led to their extinction.

Answer to "Think About It" Question

(Page 40)   The Bushmen used the large empty eggs of ostriches to carry water.

Answers to "Thought/Discussion" Questions

(Page 43)

1. Answers will vary, but scientists and others have theories about the purposes of the rock art, including the following:

   a. Some people believe that rock art was a kind of magic that put a spell over the animals painted so that they would be easier to kill.

   b. Another reason for rock art could have been to record an event that the Bushmen wanted to remember, like a dance, hunt, or the first time they saw a white man.

   c. It is, of course, possible that the art was done for the pure pleasure it gave the artist.

2. Answers will vary.   3. Answers will vary.

Bibliography

Adult Books

Lewis-Williams, J. David. *The Rock Art of Southern Africa.* Cambridge, UK: Cambridge, 1983.

Ritchie, Carson I.A. *Rock Art of Africa.* London: A.S. Barnes and Co., 1979.

Wannenburgh, Alf. *The Bushmen.* New York: Mayflower Books, 1979.

Willcox, A.R. *The Rock Art of Africa.* London: Croom Helm, 1984.

Juvenile Books

Helfman, Elizabeth S. *The Bushmen and Their Stories.* New York: Seabury Press, 1971.

Seed, Jenny. *The Bushman's Dream: African Tales of the Creation.* Scarsdale, NY: Bradbury Press, 1975.

Magazine Articles

Goodman, David. "Africa's Oldest Survivors," *World Monitor,* Vol. 6, No. 4 (April 1993), pp. 38–44.

Solomon, Anne. "Rock Art in Southern Africa," *Scientific American,* Vol. 275, No. 5 (November 1996), pp. 106–113.

CHAPTER 4:
Rock Art Wonders of the Bushmen

AFRICA

④ The focus of this chapter is the rock art and culture of the Bushmen, who were living in southern Africa at least 20,000 years ago.

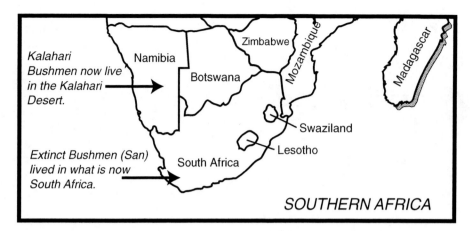

SOUTHERN AFRICA

Wonders of Rock Art

The Bushmen (also called San) are an ancient race of people who live in Africa. They are hunter-gatherers, which means they hunt wild animals and gather wild plants to survive.

For perhaps thousands of years the Bushmen who lived in southern Africa painted pictures on the walls of rock shelters and engraved pictures on the surface of stone hills or outcroppings. The engravings are called petroglyphs.

The artists' pictures showed many details of their lives—the animals they hunted, the dances they danced, and their religious beliefs. The carefully blended reds and whites of the paintings and the finely detailed engravings are a treasure of primitive art.

All of the Bushmen of southern Africa—those who created the paintings and petroglyphs—are now extinct. The only Bushmen who still survive live in the Kalahari Desert, which stretches across part of Namibia and Botswana. Some of these Bushmen are still hunter-gatherers, and their beliefs and activities are similar to the extinct Bushmen. But they do not paint or engrave because in the desert, they do not have rock surfaces on which to create art.

Hunters

The paintings and carvings of the southern Bushmen show how they hunted and killed animals for food and skins. One painting shows a dying eland (large antelope) with a broken spear in its leg. As it staggers, it is being followed by hunters and their dogs. In other pictures, hunters stalk game with bows and arrows. They are also shown scraping and cleaning animal skins, which are spread out and staked to the ground.

A Bushman artist must have spent many days punching out bits of rock to make this picture of an eland. It is not known why artists would use this method of making art rather than the less time-consuming method of painting.

People who saw the last southern Bushmen in the 1800's reported that the hunters used poison arrows. The deadly poison was probably made from plants or snake venom. Rock art paintings show the hunters carrying the arrows stuck in a band around their heads, so they could quickly pull them out and shoot them.

After the animal was struck with an arrow, the shaft would fall off, leaving the poisoned tip in the animal's body. Sometimes it took days for the animal to die, so the hunters had to be very good at following its tracks. Many rock paintings and carvings show animal hoofprints. This may have been a way for the Bushmen to train young hunters to follow game.

Bushmen are also known to trap animals and to fish. Rock artists painted scenes that show men in boats encircling a large school of fish. The men are standing in the boats holding what look like very long, thin spears that they are using to stab at the fish.

Dancers and Trancers

The San men and women of the Kalahari believe that by dancing and going into trance, they can become full of power. They wear dancing rattles made of seed pods filled with small stones.

When they are powerful through trance, they believe they can draw sickness out of people and into their own bodies, then sneeze it out violently, which causes nosebleeds.

Kalahari medicine men also dance and go into trance to gain the power to lead animals into the traps of waiting hunters. They wear antelope ears to trick the god Kaggen, who watches over antelope.

Another reason that the Kalahari medicine men go into trance is to gain the power to lead a "rain animal" over dry land and bring much-needed rain. At the end of a dance they kill the animal, believing that its blood and milk become rain.

The rock paintings of the extinct southern Bushmen show similar dances and scenes of people going into trance. White flecks in paintings may be symbols for the power that surrounds the medicine men during trance.

Rock paintings show medicine men dancing to drive out sickness. In one picture a figure is lying down while others hold sticks and dance around him in a circle. Others are shown with arms raised. Some medicine men have dots painted below their noses, probably showing that blood is dripping, as they "sneeze out" sickness and evil.

In other paintings, medicine men wear antelope ears to try to trick Kaggen into thinking they are ante-

The rock painting on top left shows an archer with poison-tipped arrows around his head. The top right painting shows trance dancers. The lines coming from the heads may be headdresses or the spirits of the dancers leaving their bodies. The painting on the bottom is a Bushman riding a horse. (Archer illustration: Dover Publications, Inc.)

lope as they lead an animal into a trap.

Southern Bushmen also believed they could gain the power to bring rain. In one painting they are leading a "rain animal" by a rope and carrying sweet-smelling herbs to calm it.

Sometimes the supernatural power that medicine men achieved is shown in rock paintings by a line or a swarm of bees. In one painting three women are linked together by a line of power as they clap their hands, dance, and sing medicine songs. The importance of the hands is shown by the careful drawing of all the fingers.

Bushmen today sometimes dance and play musical instruments just for their own entertainment, not as part of a ceremony. Rock paintings may also show people playing musical instruments, although scientists do not agree on this. One scene shows a seated person holding something that looks like it has three strings. Dots float above the strings. One observer believed it showed a man smoking, with the dots being the puffs of smoke. Another person believed the painting showed a man playing a musical bow, with the dots being the notes of the music. Bushmen have been seen playing instruments that consist of strings on a bow.

Animals

Animals were very important to the southern Bushmen who hunted them for meat, used their skin for clothes and bags, and their eggs for carrying water. That is why so many animals are shown in rock art.

Colors were blended carefully to create the natural shape of the pictured animal's shoulder and belly. Sometimes animals are painted as if seen from the front or rear. The paintings show many details, including eyes, nose, mouth, and horns.

Wild animals that the San painted and carved included the eland, elephant, giraffe, ostrich, crane, wildebeest, oryx, springbok, bushpig, and rhinoceros.

The Bushmen believed that eland had supernatural power. Many times they painted an eland close to death with its head hung down and staring, hollow eyes. Some scientists believe this was a symbol of the deathlike trance of the medicine men when they were trying to achieve power to cure the problems of their people.

Other artwork includes a zebra that can be seen on a rock outcropping. The outline of its body and its stripes were made with thousands of tiny dots pecked into the rock with a chisel and stone hammer.

Baboons are also pictured in Bushmen rock art. Their hopping around may be associated with the dancing that medicine men do. The people believed that baboons taught medicine men their songs.

Sometimes paintings show animals that are now extinct, like the great buffalo and a type of hartebeest.

The Coming of the White Race

When the white race started moving into southern Africa, in the 1700's, the Bushmen's way of life was threatened.

As they had done for thousands of years, the Bushmen moved around the countryside looking for wild animals and plants to eat. The Europeans wanted the land for grazing cattle. Because Caucasians took the lands they had always lived on, the Bushmen were forced to move on, to mountainous areas where there

The Bushmen artists painted supernatural animals from stories, such as the two-headed snake on the top. The other two animals—the bushpig in the center and the eland on the bottom—are animals seen in the everyday lives of the Bushmen. (Snake illustration: Dover Publications, Inc.)

wasn't much food. They stole cattle to survive. The Caucasians saw them as criminals and executed them whenever possible.

Rock artists painted their experiences with Europeans. In one large scene, white men on horseback are shooting at Bushmen who are trying to steal cattle. The Bushmen run away with legs flung out to show rapid movement. The scene includes many details, including the white smoke from the gun and the reins hanging down as the horse waits for his rider.

Later rock art shows European ships with masts, horses and wagons, and even European women in wide skirts. In one scene, a British soldier in uniform is leading his horse with the reins over his elbow, as was the custom of the time. No doubt the Bushmen were amazed and troubled by what they saw.

These Bushmen are now extinct, but it is possible to make a connection with them by looking at their artwork. They signed their paintings with handprints by covering their hand with paint and pressing it onto the surface of the rock wall. Perhaps if we place our hand upon the handprint on the cave wall, we can connect with the Bushmen of long ago and gain a little of their power and spirit.

Think About It—

The Bushmen used the large egg of an animal to carry water. Can you guess which animal's egg was used for this purpose? (Hint: It was mentioned in the reading.)

Wonders of World Cultures—Exploring Africa

Name _____

Date _____

Making a Rock Picture

For thousands of years, Bushmen (also called San) artists of southern Africa painted on the walls of rock shelters. Many of these paintings are still there. The paintings have lasted because the artists used plant and mineral paints that bonded with the rock surface.

The artists usually painted scenes from their everyday life—hunting, fishing, herds of animals passing by, medicine men and women dancing and going into trance, fighting other Bushmen with bows and arrows. In the 1800's the Bushmen began to paint white men chasing them and shooting at them. Many of the things the Bushmen artists painted remain a mystery to modern viewers.

- ◆ *Objective:* To create a "rock" art scene
- ◆ *Time to Complete Activity:* 2–3 hours
- ◆ *Materials Needed:* A section of light-colored concrete (sidewalk, driveway, etc.), sidewalk chalk, tempera paint, large paintbrush

Directions:

— In your group, decide what activity you want to draw.

— Before you start drawing, decide who will draw which figures and where the figures will be drawn on your section of concrete.

— Sketch each figure roughly with chalk.

— If the group is satisfied with the rough organization of the scene, finish each figure by making a more detailed outline and then filling in the outline. Remember, the drawings will have to be simplified somewhat.

— "Sign" your artwork by making handprints (paint tempera on one of your hands and press it to the concrete, or place your hand on the concrete and blow or spray paint around your hand to create a reverse image).

The eland was one of the most important animals in the life of the San people of southern Africa. On their rock canvases, the San artists skillfully captured the eland's movements and delicate coloring.

Name _____

Date _____

Making a Rock Engraving (Petroglyph)

For thousands of years, Bushmen (also called San) artists of southern Africa made engravings (petroglyphs) on the surface of rock outcroppings. They created realistic, detailed scenes of animals. They also engraved pictures of humans and geometric figures, like circles, suns, and parallel lines. No one really knows what these figures meant to the Bushmen.

Stone carving is a very difficult and time-consuming way to create pictures. One way the Bushmen did it was to scratch designs on rock walls with a sharp, pointed stone. The stone would have to be resharpened very often.

Another method of making a petroglyph was to scratch an outline of the subject then fill it in and create detail by chipping or pecking out thousands of tiny dots of rock.

- ◆ *Objective:* To make a petroglyph
- ◆ *Time to Complete Activity:* 2–3 hours
- ◆ *Materials Needed:* A hard rock with one flat side, a $\frac{3}{23}$ rock punch (available at hardware stores) or a large, case-hardened nail, high-quality standard-size hammer, safety goggles, chalk, gardening gloves (optional)

Directions:

— Choose a simple design that you would like to engrave on the rock.

— Make an outline of the design with chalk.

— Put on the safety goggles and gloves. Make sure no one is close to you while you are working.

— Working outside, chip out small bits of the rock along the outline. To do this, hold the punch (or nail) firmly against the rock and strike the punch sharply several times with the hammer. Occasionally, brush away rock dust so you can see your design better.

— After you have finished the outline, make any details by chipping out more small bits of rock.

San artists used many of these patterns of a sun with rays in their rock engravings.

Name _____

Date _____

Thought/Discussion Questions

1. After reading this chapter, what is your opinion or theory about why the Bushmen painted and carved pictures on rock surfaces?

_____

_____

_____

_____

_____

2. If you were a hunter-gatherer, what animals could you hunt and what plants could you gather to eat in your community?

_____

_____

_____

_____

3. In a painting or a carving, how would you show that someone had achieved great power and radiated this power from his or her body—as if it were something that could be touched or seen?

_____

_____

_____

_____

_____

CHAPTER 5: *Brass Wonders of the Warrior Kingdom of Benin*

Chapter Summary

What are the "wonders" in this story?

The wonders in this story are the brass sculptures rediscovered by Europeans in the late 1800's.

What are the major themes about the kingdom of Benin covered in the story and activities in this chapter?

- The warrior kingdom of Benin that developed in the Middle Ages in what is now southwestern Nigeria was ruled by a series of divine kings, called *obas*.

- The people of Benin, who are called the *Edo*, learned the art of brass casting and produced many articles made of brass, including heads (busts), plaques, statues, and shrines.
- The brass items made by the Edo have symbolic and spiritual meaning for them.
- Trade with the Portuguese and other Europeans in the Middle Ages produced great wealth for the oba and his people.
- Contact with the British in the late 1800's was disastrous for the oba and the people of Benin.

Answer to "Think About It" Question

(page 54)

In the past, tamed leopards would walk beside the oba in parades to show that the oba had tamed the king of the forest.

Answers to "Thought/Discussion" Questions

(page 59)

1. Answers will vary.
2. Answers will vary.
3. Answers will vary.

Bibliography

Adult Books

Ben-Amos, Paula. *The Art of Benin.* Washington, DC: Smithsonian Institution Press, 1995.

Bradbury, R.E. *Benin Studies.* London: International African Institute, 1973.

Dark, Philip J.C. *An Introduction to Benin Art and Technology.* Oxford: Oxford University Press, 1973.

Duchâteau, Armand. *Benin: Royal Art from the Museum für Völkerkunde, Vienna.* Munich: Prestel-Verlag, 1994.

Kaplan, Flora S. *Images of Power: Art of the Royal Court of Benin.* New York: New York University, 1981.

Koslow, Philip. *Benin: Lords of the River.* New York: Chelsea House Publishers, 1996.

Juvenile Books

Koslow, Philip. *Benin: Lords of the River.* New York: Chelsea House Publishers, 1996.

CHAPTER 5:
Brass Wonders of the Warrior Kingdom of Benin

AFRICA

⑤ *The focus of this chapter is the medieval kingdom of Benin, about* A.D. *1400–1900.*

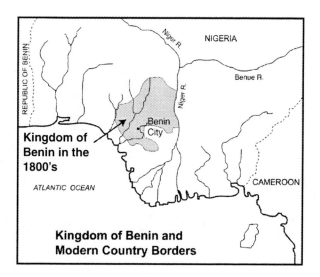

Kingdom of Benin in the 1800's

ATLANTIC OCEAN

Kingdom of Benin and Modern Country Borders

Treasures Rediscovered by the British in 1897

In the second half of the 1800's, Britain was trying to trade with Africans along the coast near the kingdom of Benin. (See map above.) The British wanted the king of Benin, called the **oba**, to agree to let them control and protect the area. It took several years but finally the oba reluctantly agreed to the British demands.

The oba continued to resist the British by blocking shipments of goods that were leaving Africa to go to markets in Europe. The local British official decided that he could not allow the oba to do as he pleased. The official and an expedition of about 200 started out to visit the oba. Warriors attacked the expedition and killed almost everyone.

The next month, February 1897, Britain sent a force of 1,500 against the oba and took over Benin City. The city was almost deserted because the oba and his warriors, chiefs, and family had already left.

In August, the oba publicly surrendered to the British by rubbing his forehead three times on the ground, as was the local custom. The British learned that palace chiefs, not the oba, had given the order to destroy their expedition. The chiefs were sentenced to death. The oba was forced to live the rest of his life away from his homeland.

In the royal palace that the oba left behind the British found royal treasures—several hundred brass plaques, some items of ivory, brass statues and heads, and brass stools. These works of art had powerful meaning to the people of Benin, who called themselves and their kingdom **Edo**. By taking the items, the British hoped that the power of the oba would be broken, and the Edo people could be controlled more easily. Thus, the magnificent brass works of art were taken back to London and sold, eventually to be scattered all over the world.

Brass Artworks Tell the Story of the Warrior Kingdom of Benin

By the fifteenth to sixteenth century Benin was a warrior kingdom that had conquered many of its neighbors.

Brass Heads

Some of the heads were trophies of war. It was the custom in ancient Benin to cut off the heads of the most stubborn of the captured kings. The oba would then have the heads cast in brass and sent back to the beheaded king's son to remind him of what could also happen to him.

Head of Queen Mother Idia

who helped her son, the oba, win a war. Her hairstyle is called "chicken's beak" and is covered with a beaded cap.

Edo craftsmen also made brass heads of the oba when he died. The heads would be placed in an altar (shrine) to the oba to honor and remember him. Because the mother of the oba was also a powerful person, a brass head would be cast for her too when she died.

In the late 1400's, Portuguese traders came to the coast of Benin looking for products to trade and trying to convert the Africans to Christianity. A Portuguese sailor wrote about how the people of Benin worshiped their kings (obas). The kings would not allow their people to see them eating, because that might destroy the belief that the kings were godlike and could exist without food.

The oba became very strong and rich because he was able to control African trade with Europeans. With the help of the Portuguese, he conquered most of his neighbors and became even stronger.

The Portuguese also supplied luxury items, like coral beads and brass that could be melted down to make works of art. In return, the Edo supplied the Portuguese with pepper, cloth, ivory, and slaves.

Plaque of a Chief

He wears a bell around his neck as a symbol of protection in battle. He would ring it on the way home to announce victory. The face of a leopard on his chest is also for protection. It is supposed to frighten the enemy in battle.

The brass heads began to show the increase in wealth and importance of the oba. Precious and expensive ivory tusks were placed into the top of the heads and huge numbers of brass and coral beads decorate the heads.

After a period of civil war in the 1600's, the oba conquered rebellious local chiefs who wanted to be king. With strong leadership and increased trade with the Dutch, Benin again was prosperous. The Dutch mainly wanted ivory from the Edo, and the Edo wanted luxury items from the Dutch. They traded for cowrie shells, which were used like money, French silk and linen, and a huge number of brass and copper pans. The brass pans were probably melted down to make brass heads and other artworks. Heads of this period are practically covered with expensive coral beads—row after row of coral necklaces are stacked up to form a collar of beads.

Brass Plaques

The Benin plaques are sheets of brass that have figures of men or animals cast into them. The Portuguese may have inspired the Edo craftsmen to start making plaques, possibly by showing them books with pictures.

Many of the plaques tell something about life at the court of the oba. For instance, people who came to visit the oba—such as Edo officials, Europeans, messengers, warriors, and musicians—would be shown on plaques.

Objects or designs on the plaques are supposed to protect the person depicted from harm. High-ranking warriors would be shown with leopards' heads that were supposed to frighten the enemy.

One of the plaques shows a Portuguese soldier holding a stick with a burning fuse on one end that was used to light a cannon from a safe distance. This was probably one of the ways the Portuguese helped the Edo fight their enemies—with cannons!

Musicians with small rattles made from gourds and a flute player are shown on plaques. They probably entertained the oba and his family.

Plaques with animals show how the Edo people thought that certain animals had special powers. Crocodiles and snakes were special, because they live both on land and in water and serve as a bridge between the two. The land is represented by the oba, and the water is represented by Olokun, the Edo god of waters. The Edo believed that Olokun sometimes sent snakes and crocodiles to punish people who had done bad things.

The leopard is another animal that appears on plaques and was special to the Edo. He represents the two forces that the ideal leader, the oba, should have—the cruel force that frightens and the calm force that leads.

Birds and fish also appear on plaques. All of the fish are varieties of mudfish (or catfish) that are greatly valued by the Edo as the strongest and best tasting of all fish. Some kinds of mudfish can close their gills and "walk" across land for great distances. Thus, they are a symbol for the oba who could also overcome obstacles.

Statues

The oldest and most mysterious figures found by the British in Benin City are the two statues of dwarfs. They seem to be realistic figures of people who were very short, had large heads, long chests, and short legs and arms. Some who have studied Benin culture say the dwarfs might have been acrobats and jugglers at the court of the oba, but no one knows for sure. Tests revealed that these figures are almost 700 years old, dating from about 1324.

There are also statues of animals, including the rooster, which was part of the altar of the queen mother (the mother of the oba). The rooster probably represented the male powers that were given to the queen mother—such as her own palace, money, people to serve her, and the use of magic forces when she needed them.

The Edo craftsmen made statues of Portuguese soldiers, including an archer shooting a crossbow. His hat, clothes, and the crossbow are typical of European styles from the 1500's.

The Kingdom of Benin Today

After the British took over Benin City, in 1897, the kingdom of Benin was never again independent. However, in 1914 the British allowed the oldest son of the last oba to come back to Benin and take over as king of the Edo people. This new king again encouraged craftsmen to make beautiful objects out of brass and other materials. He had these artists make replace-ments for the pieces that had been taken by the British. He even allowed the products to be sold to outsiders.

Benin, located just west of Nigeria, was first a British colony. In 1960, it became an independent nation.

The Edo people continue to practice their rituals and create their works of art, and the oba still reigns over his kingdom.

A Portuguese Soldier

After contact with Europeans, Benin brass artists began to make brass images of European soldiers, including their weapons.

Think About It—

After reading about the oba, can you guess which animal would walk beside him in parades?

Symbols of Protection and Communication

The Edo people of the medieval kingdom of Benin believed (and still believe) in a spirit world where Osanobua, the god who created the world, lives. Other gods and spirits also live there and can cross over to the physical world to hurt people or help them. Olukun, the most popular god in Benin, is associated with water. He also brings wealth, success, and children. Parents of a girl child will set up a shrine to Olukun and ask him to protect her.

The most evil spirits are called *azen* (witches). They live in the treetops of the forest and send out their evil powers in the form of a vicious bird who sucks life out of victims, transforms the life into a goat or antelope, then eats it. Some people in Ebo society claim they can get rid of azen through the power of an iron staff they carry. The staff represents flames shooting up that drive away the evil witches.

◆ *Objective:* As part of a cultural display, create protective or communication symbols for your classroom.
◆ *Time to Complete Activity:* 1–2 hours
◆ *Materials Needed:* See below for each symbol.

Directions:

___ Choose one of the protection or communication symbols below to make for your classroom as a cultural display. Several students may want to work together to make some of the objects.

1. **To protect against evil:** Palm fronds woven with streamers of red cloth and decorated with small mirrors and pieces of brass are worn in dances to purify and protect the village.

2. **To protect against evil:** Whips made of forked sticks can be seen on brass artworks from Benin. These whips are waved in the air to drive away evil spirits.

3. **To protect against evil:** Bells decorated with designs of mudfish (catfish), crocodiles, water tortoises, and snakes are rung to drive away evil spirits. These animals all live in Olukun's pure and perfect world and are able to counter evil forces. The bells that the Edo use look like cowbells. If you don't have a cowbell, use any bell and decorate with the designs below (or use your own designs).

4. **To communicate with spirits:** Rattle staffs are struck on the ground to call spirits of ancestors or to ask a god to enter one's body. You can make a rattle staff out of a long piece of bamboo with small stones inside to cause the rattle. Seal both ends with masking tape and decorate with design below (or use your own designs).

Bell Designs

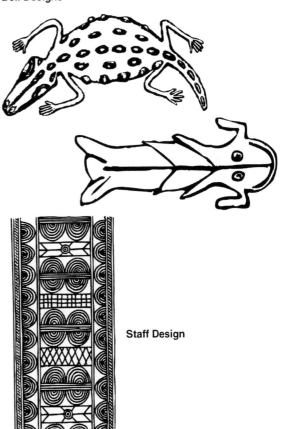

Staff Design

Name _____

Date _____

Making a Pangolin Hat

The Edo people of the medieval African kingdom of Benin were ruled by a king called the oba. In the past, high-ranking chiefs, called town chiefs, were responsible for collecting gifts for the oba, finding soldiers to fight the oba's battles, and many other duties. They were very often in conflict with the oba. During rituals they dressed in elaborate costumes called *pangolin skin*. They still do. This costume imitates the scales of the pangolin, or scaly anteater, which curls up when attacked and cannot be killed easily. The town chiefs chose this costume because not even the leopard, which represents the oba, can kill the pangolin.

- ◆ *Objective:* To make a pangolin hat
- ◆ *Time to Complete Activity:* 2 hours
- ◆ *Materials Needed:* Poster board (at least 17 inches square), pencil, 24-inch length of string, scissors, masking tape, glue, red felt or other red fabric

Directions:

— Make an X-mark on the posterboard about $\frac{1}{4}$ inch from one corner.

— From the center of the X-mark, measure and mark $15\frac{7}{8}$ inches along each of the edges adjoining the corner.

— About 3 inches from the tip, tie the pencil to one end of the string.

— Hold the tip of the pencil (that is attached to one end of the string) on one of the $15\frac{7}{8}$ inch marks. With your other hand, pull the other end of the string to the X-mark. You will have to adjust the positions of your hands so that the string is extended fairly tightly from the X-mark to the 15-7/8 inch mark.

— Hold the string securely at the X-mark, and with the pencil at the other end of the string, draw an arc (curved line) from the first $15\frac{7}{8}$ inch mark to the other $15\frac{7}{8}$ inch mark.

— Cut along the arc from edge to edge so that you have a triangle shape that is curved on one edge.

— To make the cone-shaped hat, fold the straight edges of the shape together, overlap them about $\frac{1}{2}$ inch, and secure with masking tape.

— Using the scale pattern below, cut many pangolin scales out of the red felt.

— Cut out four red flaps that are nearly as long as the hat itself. (Look at the sketch below to get an idea of the proportion.)

— Glue the scales onto the cone hat in rows, starting at the bottom, and overlapping the rows.

— Glue the flaps onto the edges of the cone hat as shown below.

Variation: Use the pangolin hat in an African cultural display or festival. (While you are wearing the hat, watch out for leopards!)

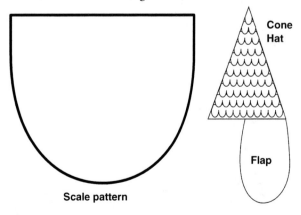

Scale pattern

Cone Hat

Flap

Wonders of World Cultures—Exploring Africa

Name _____

Date _____

Creation Stories

The Edo people of the medieval kingdom of Benin have a story about how the world was created by their god. In the beginning, they say, there was no land, only water. God decided to put people in the world, so he sent his three sons off in canoes. He told them they could each have a wish before they left. The two oldest sons asked for wealth and tools to make crafts. Before the youngest son could name his wish, his father gave him a snail shell. When the youngest son reached the center of the waters, he turned the snail shell upside down. Out came sand in a continuous stream. It eventually piled up enough to create all of the land. God came down to the land on a chain and sent people down the chain to live in all parts of the world. God's youngest son became the first king of the kingdom of Benin.

◆ *Objective:* To research other creation stories
◆ *Time to Complete Activity:* 1–2 hours
◆ *Materials Needed:* Research materials, paper, pencil

Directions:

___ Read about the creation stories of several other cultures. Summarize them to the right in your own words.

Variation: Write a play based on one of the creation stories, and act it out with other students.

Creation Stories

_____
_____
_____
_____
_____
_____
_____
_____
_____
_____
_____
_____
_____
_____
_____
_____
_____
_____
_____

Name _____

Date _____

Thought/Discussion Questions

1. Why do you think the British of the late 1800's thought they had the right to control trade along the coast near Benin City?

   _____

   _____

   _____

   _____

2. The Edo believe that animals have certain powers, or qualities. For instance, a leopard can be cruel but also calm—two qualities that make a good leader, according to the Edo. They also believe that a mudfish is very persistent, another quality of a good leader. In your culture, which animals have qualities that people want to have? List those animals and their qualities. (For instance, lions are thought to be fierce and strong, so a football team may name themselves the "Hometown Lions" to show how strong they are—and perhaps put fear into the hearts of the opposing team.)

   _____

   _____

   _____

   _____

   _____

3. The Edo remember their past through an oral tradition rather than through writing. It is the duty of the oba, some of the priests, some craftsmen, and a few others to remember the list of obas, the obas' wars and adventures, and their artistic achievements. They retell these events in stories. Can you think of occasions in your own life when people tell stories about their achievements and adventures? How is this storytelling different from the stories the Edo tell about the obas?

   _____

   _____

   _____

   _____

CHAPTER 6: *Wonders of the Asante Empire of Gold*

Chapter Summary

What are the "wonders" in this story?

The Asante empire, its gold, and its treasured objects, many made of gold

What are the major themes about the Asante empire covered in this chapter?

- The Asante economy of the 1800's was based largely on gold.
- Europeans "discovered" the Asante empire and the Gold Coast of western Africa in the fifteenth century. Eventually, they wanted to control this trade in gold and other products.

- The British and the Asante fought a series of wars that ended in 1900 with the destruction of the Asante nation.

- The British did not understand Asante traditions and beliefs. They thought the Asante were blood-thirsty warriors who wanted nothing but war, which was untrue.

Answer to "Think About It" Question

(page 66)

Visitors to the Asante kingdom reported that slaves worked in gold mines, served as servants in the king's palace, and worked on street and building construction projects. Of course, they may have performed many other jobs that were not reported by visitors.

Answers to "Thought/Discussion" Questions

(page 63)   1–3. Answers will vary.

Answer to "Units of Weight Measurement"

(page 68)

Standard Set of Brass Weights (based on 1.46 gram unit)	
Weight of Each Brass Weight	**Amount of Gold Dust Needed to Balance Weight**
3 units	4.38 grams
4 units	5.85 grams
4.5 units	6.67 grams
6 units	8.76 grams
8 units	11.68 grams
9 units	13.14 grams
10 units	14.6 grams
11 units	16.06 grams
12 units	17.52 grams
24 units	35.04 grams
36 units	52.56 grams
48 units	70.08 grams

Answer to **Variation:** One combination of weights you could use is one weight that weighs 14.60 grams (10 × 1.46 grams) plus one that weighs 35.04 grams (24 × 1.46 grams). Can you think of other combinations of weights?

Bibliography

Adult Books

Edgerton, Robert B. *The Fall of the Asante Empire: The Hundred-Year War for Africa's Gold Coast.* New York: The Free Press, 1995.

Freeman, Richard A. *Travels and Life in Ashanti and Jaman.* London: Archibald Constable & Co., 1898.

McLeod, M.D. *The Asante.* London: British Museum Publications Ltd., 1981.

Ward, W.E.F. *A History of the Gold Coast.* London: George Allen & Unwin Ltd., 1948.

Juvenile Books

Daaku, Yeboa K. *Osei Tutu of Asante.* London: Heinemann Educational Books Ltd., 1976.

Magazine Articles

Beckwith, Carol, and Angela Fisher. "Royal Gold of the Asante Empire," *National Geographic,* Vol. 190, No. 4 (October, 1996) pp. 36–47.

Wonders of the Asante Empire of Gold

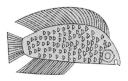

AFRICA

⑥ *The focus of this chapter is the Asante empire of the 1800's.*

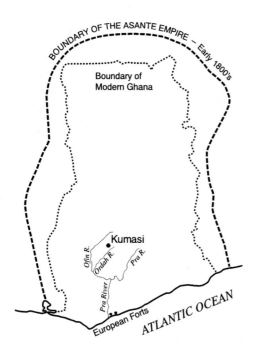

BOUNDARY OF THE ASANTE EMPIRE – Early 1800's

Boundary of
Modern Ghana

• Kumasi

Ofin R.

Ordah R.

Pra R.

Pra River

European Forts

ATLANTIC OCEAN

First Visit by Englishmen

The lure of gold finally outweighed the Europeans' fear of going into the interior of western Africa. In 1817 a small group of Englishmen visited the Asante king Osei Bonsu. They were dazzled by all the gold they saw. Asante officers and chiefs had large lumps of gold tied to their wrists and life-size, solid-gold wolves' heads attached to their swords. The king had a gold ring on every finger. He wore a green silk robe and carried gold clackers that he would click together when he wanted those around him to be silent. Near the king, under an umbrella, was the golden stool—a stool completely covered with gold. No one could sit on it, not even the king. It was said to hold the soul of the Asante people and protect them from harm.

Treasured Objects of the Asante People

Swords.   Swords were carried as symbols of the status or achievement of their owners. Two of the king's wives would stand behind him carrying on their shoulders large gold sabers. The generals in the king's army all had gold-handled swords given to them by the king. Some special swords were thought to have powers of protection and were laid beside the king as he slept.

Staffs.   Europeans who wanted to communicate with the Asante helped to introduce the use of staffs into their culture. The staffs were usually plain wooden sticks with gold or silver tops. Since the Asante could neither read nor write, the Europeans needed a way to show the king that the messenger coming to talk to him had the full authority or backing of the Europeans. Carrying the white man's staff was a way to show this authority.

Stools.   Asante people sat on stools during all kinds of activities—men would sit on them while weaving and women would sit on them while cooking on the home fire.

Stools also had meaning beyond these common activities. About 30 different types of stools were made in Asante society. Some designs could only be used by people of certain ranks. For instance, stools that had a

A Kingdom of Gold

European traders started coming to the coast of western Africa in the 1400's. The Portuguese called it the Gold Coast because of all the specks of gold they saw floating in the rivers and streams.

Traders would bring things the Africans wanted, like glass beads and cloth. The Africans would, in turn, give the Europeans something they wanted, like palm oil, ivory, and slaves.

The Europeans, of course, were looking for gold, but they did not know about the **Asante empire** of gold until the late 1600's. The Asante empire was inland, where the Europeans were afraid to go. This fear kept them in their forts on the coast.

The Asante people, whose capital was at Kumasi (see map above), kept millions of dollars worth of gold dust in their government treasury. Gold dust was used by the Asante as money to buy what they needed.

Some of the gold was found in streams. It was panned mostly by women and children. Most of the gold, however, was dug out of the ground. In a good year, as many as 40,000 shallow pits and a few very deep ones were being mined all over the Asante empire.

leopard or elephant design could only be used by the king, because these animals were symbols of his greatness and fierceness.

The greatest stool was the golden stool. According to tradition, this stool came from the sky for Osei Tutu, the king who united the Asante into a nation.

Brass Weights, Spoons for Gold Dust, and Boxes for Gold Dust. The Asante people used gold dust as money, so they had to have a set of weights for weighing the dust, spoons for scooping it up, and special boxes for carrying it.

The measurement system that the Asante used probably came from Islamic people that they traded with. The weights, which were made of brass, could measure gold dust from very small to very large amounts. A weight was placed on one side of a scale, and the amount of gold dust needed to balance the weight was scooped into the other side of the scale.

The brass weights were works of art in themselves. The designs on them tell a lot about Asante life. Men are shown after a day of hunting, with the game slung

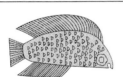

Brass weights used to weigh gold were made to show many activities, sometimes funny scenes, of Asante daily life.

over their shoulders. Women are shown carrying bundles of wood on their heads or pounding a local food called *fu-fu*. Warriors or executioners are holding severed heads of criminals or enemies killed in battle. Priests can be seen dancing with shrines on their heads or sacrificing chickens.

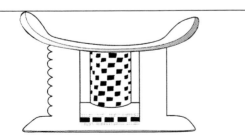

Most of the stools in Asante society were made of a light-colored wood. They were cleaned with water and fine river sand before any major ceremony. (Drawing from Travels and Life in Ashanti and Jaman, *by R.A. Freeman. London: Archibald Constable & Co., 1898.)*

When the Asante came into contact with Europeans, their brass weights began to show objects from Europe—like cannon, locks, keys, handguns, and pipes for smoking tobacco.

Because gold dust might stick to fingers, brass spoons were used to scoop it up. The handles of the spoons were decorated with geometric designs.

Brass boxes were used to carry gold dust. The lids were decorated with designs and pictures just like the ones on weights. Gold dust was stored in the boxes in little squares of cloth, twisted and tied at the neck.

Some of the People of the Asante Empire

Classes of People. The English visitors only saw the upper class of people in Asante society. The men of this class were more than six feet tall and very strong. The women were beautiful, gentle, and wore fine clothes, according to one of the Englishmen.

There were also lower classes of people, mainly slaves from conquered neighboring kingdoms.

People Who Shared Power with the King. On the surface it looked as if the king was the head of the government and the most powerful person in Asante, but actually he shared power with a group of about 200 men who came from all over the empire. In addition there were 18 other people who advised the king and sometimes forced him to do things. This council was called the Asante Porcupine, because no one could touch them. It included military generals, the government treasurer, the chief doctor, a high priest, and the king's own mother. They met almost every day to decide all kinds of matters.

Priests. The Asante people believed in a god who had created the world. They also believed in many lesser gods. When a person died, according to Asante religious beliefs, the soul went to the underworld. There it kept track of the living; it rewarded those who followed the laws of Asante society and punished those who didn't.

The priests helped people deal with bad things that happened to them, with sickness, and with death. It was believed that the priests got their power from *mmoatia,* dwarfs who lived in the forest and looked like little people.

Executioners. On the first day of the Englishmen's visit, the royal executioner was introduced to them. He was a huge man who wore a gold chest plate. He shook the blood-soaked executioner's stool at them as a warning not to break Asante law.

Criminals were executed in front of large crowds. People were also sacrificed for religious purposes. Many of them were slaves from conquered tribes.

Police. In addition to executioners, there were police in Kumasi. It was easy to identify them. They wore their hair long and carried whips, knives, and muskets. One of their jobs was to stand on the edge of town and make sure no one entered or left Kumasi without permission from the government. They patrolled the borders of the Asante empire to keep the peace. They questioned travelers about their business and arrested criminals.

How People Lived

Houses. In Kumasi, people lived in neat one- or two-story houses decorated with red clay designs. They were kept very clean. Most of the larger buildings had indoor toilets that were flushed with boiling water. Houses faced onto wide, tree-shaded streets that were swept clean every day. Household trash was collected and burned every day, too.

Food and Other Necessities. Large markets in Kumasi sold everything people needed, including beef, mutton, wild hog, antelope, monkey, and large smoked snails. Vegetables, fruits, eggs, sugar cane, tobacco, beer, and palm wine were also available. Nonfood products included beads, sandals, silk and cotton cloth, and gunpowder.

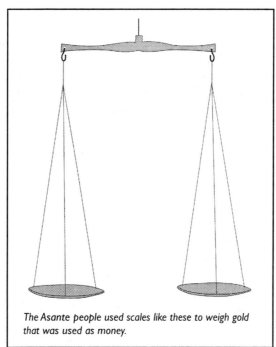

The Asante people used scales like these to weigh gold that was used as money.

Village Life. Not everyone lived in Kumasi. Many people lived in small villages throughout the Asante empire. They were mostly farmers who grew yams, plantains, and many other crops and sold them at the markets. Men cut down trees and prepared the soil for planting crops. They also fished, hunted, and traded for the goods their families needed. Women did the daily work of tending the crops and also gathered large snails for meals. Children helped their mothers in the fields, cared for the family's chicken and goats, and watched their younger brothers and sisters.

The Asante Empire Fights the British Empire

In the 1800's the Asante got a powerful new neighbor—the British.

Britain wanted to control Gold Coast trade, which included mining gold, cutting timber, and exporting rubber. They thought the Asante people were not much more than bloodthirsty warriors who sacrificed many innocent victims in their religious ceremonies. The British did not believe that the Asante could be trusted as business partners.

The British and Asante forces fought each other off and on during most of the 1800's, even though the Asante kings tried many times to make peace.

In 1895 the British were afraid that France was trying to take some of the rich trade in gold, timber, and rubber by making a trading deal with the Asante. This was not true, but the British decided that the Asante must give in to British rule and trade only with them. In order to weaken the Asante nation, British troops marched into Kumasi and took away the king, his mother, and high-ranking officials. The soldiers looted the city, destroyed graves, and burned religious shrines.

Britain encouraged its businessmen to come to the Gold Coast to mine gold and cut timber on land that was owned by wealthy Asante. Free Asante people were forced to work as laborers in the mines and carry supplies, which made them very angry.

Finally, in 1900, the British went too far when they demanded that the Asante give them the golden stool, the sacred symbol of national unity for the Asante people. The new British governor of the Gold Coast even asked why he should not be able to sit on it! Stupidly, he did not realize that no one was allowed to sit on the golden stool, not even the king. Only three days after the governor's comment, the Asante rebellion began.

Even though the Asante did not have a king (he was still a hostage of the British), they fought hard against the British forces. Finally, however, the modern weapons of the British, including machine guns and

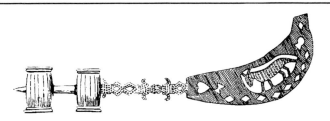

Gold sword of an Asante chief

(Drawing from Travels and Life in Ashanti and Jaman, *by R.A. Freeman. London: Archibald Constable & Co., 1898.)*

cannon, overpowered the Asante, who were still using antique muskets.

Britain controlled the Gold Coast and what once was the Asante empire until 1967, when the country of Ghana was born.

Even though the Asante people live in the nation of Ghana, they still have their own king. On special occasions he still wears gold from head to foot.

The Asante hid the golden stool from the British in 1895 and took it out of hiding in 1921. It is still placed beside the king during ceremonies as the symbol of the soul and unity of the Asante people.

Think About It—

What jobs do you think slaves performed in Asante society?

Making Kente Cloth

The Asante people, of what is now the country of Ghana, probably learned how to weave in the sixteenth century. Asante weavers, mostly men, weave narrow strips of cloth in complex patterns. Then the strips are sewn together to make a beautiful colorful cloth called *kente*. It is mostly cotton, but sometimes silk is woven with the cotton to produce areas of bright color.

◆ *Objective:* To make a small section of cloth (could be a place mat) that is like kente cloth

◆ *Time to Complete Activity:* 2–3 hours

◆ Materials Needed: Two 18-inch long × 2-inch wide, and two 13-inch long × 2-inch wide, pieces of solid color; thin cotton ribbon or fabric; many pieces of thin cotton ribbon or fabric strips in different lengths and widths in a variety of striped patterns; scissors; needle and thread; 17- × 12-inch piece of medium or heavyweight iron-on interfacing; iron; ironing board; 20- × 15-inch piece of lightweight muslin or other thin, cotton fabric; ruler; sewing machine (optional)

(Adult supervision is suggested if using a sewing machine.)

Directions:

— If necessary, iron the ribbons.

— Place the interfacing on the ironing board with the fusible side up. (Directions that come with the interfacing will tell you which side is fusible.)

— Place the two 18- × 2-inch strips along the long edges of the interfacing so that the strips extend over the edges about $\frac{1}{2}$ inch.

— Measure the distance between the two long strips and cut the 13 inch strips to fit.

— Place the strips you have just cut inside the long strips along the shorter edges of the interfacing with about $\frac{1}{2}$ inch extending over the edges.

— Place the remaining strips of fabric on the interfacing in vertical and horizontal patterns that are pleasing to you. Make sure no interfacing shows between strips.

— Lightly "tack" the strips onto the interfacing with the point of the hot iron. (Follow the directions that come with the interfacing.)

— Place the piece of muslin on top of the interfacing and strips, being careful not to move any of the strips.

— Following the directions that came with the interfacing, use the iron to fuse (or attach) the strips to the interfacing.

— Fold underneath the fabric strips that extend over the edges of the interfacing. Lightly iron the edges and sew in place by hand or machine.

Kente cloth

Wonders of World Cultures—Exploring Africa

Units of Weight Measurement

The Asante people, of what is now the country of Ghana, used gold to buy what they needed. They used scales to weigh the gold.

Once the buyer and seller agreed to the amount of gold dust needed to buy an object, a brass weight equal to that amount was put on one side of the scale. Gold dust was added to the other side of the scale until the two sides were in balance. Then the buyer would give the gold to the seller, to pay that person for the object that was being purchased.

The Asante made decorative brass weights that were small works of art. Many designs showed everyday scenes of Asante life.

Historians have studied the Asante weights and have decided that they were based on a unit equivalent to 1.46 grams.

- ◆ *Objective:* To determine the individual weights of a complete set of Asante weights in terms of the 1.46 gram unit
- ◆ *Time to Complete Activity:* 30 minutes
- ◆ *Materials Needed:* This sheet, pencil or pen

Directions:

___ Complete the table below.

Standard Set of Brass Weights (based on 1.46 gram unit)	
Weight of Each Brass Weight	**Amount of Gold Dust Needed to Balance Weight**
3 units	_____ grams
4 units	_____ grams
4.5 units	_____ grams
6 units	_____ grams
8 units	_____ grams
9 units	_____ grams
10 units	_____ grams
11 units	_____ grams
12 units	_____ grams
24 units	_____ grams
36 units	_____ grams
48 units	_____ grams

Variation: If a seller decided that the object he wanted to sell cost the equivalent of 49.65 grams of gold dust, which brass weights could be used to weigh the gold?

Making and Using a Scale

The Asante people, of what is now the country of Ghana, used gold to buy what they needed. They used scales to weigh the gold. A brass weight was put on one side of the scale, and gold dust was added to the other side of the scale until the two sides were in balance. The seller would receive the gold dust in payment for the object.

- ◆ *Objective:* To make a scale and use it

- ◆ *Time to Complete Activity:* 2–3 hours

- ◆ *Materials Needed:* 2 small aluminum pie pans, hole punch, string, pencil, 10-inch dowel, masking tape, sand, small objects that are the same weight like marbles, washers, pennies, etc.

Directions:

— Punch three holes in the same places on each pie pan with a hole punch.

— Measure $\frac{3}{4}$ inch from each end of the dowel and mark it.

— Cut two 4-inch lengths of string, and tie each one so you have two loops of string (see drawing).

— Place each loop of string on the ends of the dowel at the marks.

— Secure the string loops to the dowel with masking tape so you have a small loop of string hanging down.

— Cut six 10-inch lengths of string.

— Tie the ends of three lengths of string through the holes in each pie pan.

— Tie the other ends of the strings to the loops at the ends of the dowel.

— Measure half the distance between the loops of strings on the ends of the dowel, and place a mark there.

— Cut a 4-inch piece of string, loop it around the dowel at the mark, and tie it. Secure it with masking tape.

— Carefully hold the scale by the loop in the middle of the dowel so the pie pans hang down.

— Place one of your small objects into one of the pie pans.

— Using sand instead of gold dust, measure sand into the other pie pan until the scale is balanced.

— Use the scale to weigh sand in payment for objects that one of you is buying and one of you is selling. First, decide how much each object costs.

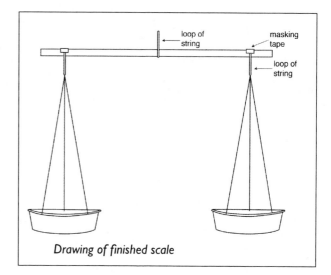

Drawing of finished scale

Thought/Discussion Questions

1. The golden stool was a sacred object to the Asante. They believed the soul and unity of their people and nation lived in the stool. They would go to war and die to protect it, if necessary. Is there an object that the people of your nation or religion think of as sacred? Please explain.

   _____

   _____

   _____

   _____

2. What do you think it would be like to buy things with gold dust?

   _____

   _____

   _____

   _____

3. The Asante were very aware of the rank of people in society. The clothes and jewelry they wore, things they carried, and even the stools they sat on showed their rank. For instance, a stool with a leopard or elephant design could only be used by the king. Do you think the people in your society are very aware of the rank of other people? What do people wear, carry, or use in their lives that shows their rank?

   _____

   _____

   _____

   _____

   _____

   _____

CHAPTER 7: *Searching for Treasure and Finding Knowledge in Central Africa*

Chapter Summary

What is the "treasure" in this story?

- Explorers of the 1800's gained a treasure of knowledge about the rivers, lakes, terrain, and people of central Africa.

What are the major themes about central Africa covered in the story and activities in this chapter?

- Non-Africans had very little information about central Africa before the 1800's.

- European traders grew rich over the centuries by buying and selling African slaves and agricultural products.

- To grow even richer, Europeans wanted to go into the interior of Africa themselves, rather than relying on African traders to bring out the goods.

- The desire to go into Africa encouraged Europeans to explore areas, such as central Africa, that had never been completely seen before by outsiders.

- In the process of exploration, Europeans (and the whole world) learned much about African geography and cultures.

Answers to "Think About It" Question

(page 70)

Stanley set out to solve the mystery of the source of the Nile River. He found that the Lualaba River is not the source of the Nile River, but becomes the Congo River.

He discovered that the source of the Nile River is Lake Victoria.

He and his expedition also mapped Lake Victoria and found that it is one large body of water rather than several small lakes.

He discovered previously unknown tribes of central Africa, many extremely unfriendly.

He discovered and wrote about the geography and weather of central Africa—the mountains, jungles, smaller rivers, falls (cataracts) on the rivers, the rain and humidity.

Answers to "Thought/Discussion" Questions

(page 74)

1. Stanley and his group had modern (for the times) guns. Most of the tribes that Stanley met did not have guns; they fought with spears and bows and arrows.

2. Answers will vary.

3. Answers will vary.

4. Within 30 years after Stanley's expedition, all of Africa was under European colonial rule.

Bibliography

Adult Books

Cohen, Daniel. *Henry Stanley and the Quest for the Source of the Nile.* New York: M. Evans, 1985.

Forbath, Peter. *The River Congo: The Discovery, Exploration and Exploitation of the World's Most Dramatic River.* New York: Harper & Row, 1977.

Hall, Richard. *Stanley: An Adventurer Explored.* Boston: Houghton Mifflin, 1975.

Jones, Constance. *Africa: 1500–1900.* New York: Facts on File, 1993.

Kamm, Josephine. *Explorers into Africa: From the Egyptians to the Victorians.* New York: Crowell, 1970.

Juvenile Books

Clinton, Susan. *The World's Great Explorers: Henry Stanley and David Livingstone.* Chicago: Children's Press, 1990.

Foster, F. Blanche. *East Central Africa: Kenya, Uganda, Tanzania, Rwanda, and Burundi.* New York: Franklin Watts, 1981.

Magazine Articles

Chadwick, Douglas H. "A Place for Parks in the New South Africa," *National Geographic,* Vol. 190, No. 1 (July 1996), pp. 2–41. (Article about conservation of animals in Africa).

Palmer, Colin. "African Slave Trade: The Cruelest Commerce," *National Geographic,* Vol. 182, No. 3 (September 1992), pp. 63–91.

CHAPTER 7: *Searching for Treasure and Finding Knowledge in Central Africa*

King Mtesa of Uganda

AFRICA

Morocco
Tunisia
Western Sahara
Algeria
Libya
Egypt
Mauritania
Mali
Niger
Chad
Sudan
Eritrea
Gambia
Senegal
Guinea-Bissau
Guinea
Burkina Faso
Nigeria
Djibouti
Sierra Leone
Ivory Coast
Ghana
Benin
Central African Republic
Ethiopia
Somalia
Liberia
Togo
Cameroon
EQUATOR
Equitorial Guinea
Gabon
Congo
Rwanda
Uganda
Kenya
Democratic Republic of Congo
Burundi
Indian Ocean
Cabinda (Angola)
Tanzania
Atlantic Ocean
Angola
Malawi
Zambia
Zimbabwe
Mozambique
Namibia
Botswana
Madagascar
Swaziland
South Africa
Lesotho

(7)

⑦ *The focus of this chapter is the exploration of central Africa from 1874–1878.*

Treasures

For centuries European traders had grown rich by trading in slaves from Africa. Most of the slaves went to markets in the Americas. European traders also bought agricultural products, especially palm oil, palm kernels, and groundnuts, from Africans, then resold these products in Europe.

By the 1800's the slave trade was disappearing. Slavery had been stopped in most countries. But Europeans still paid high prices for African palm oil and other products.

Up to that time, Africans had gone into central Africa to bring out these goods. Now, European traders wanted to go into the interior of Africa themselves. In this way they wouldn't have to pay the Africans, and they would make more money!

Another reason Europeans wanted to explore central Africa was to bring the Christian religion to more Africans.

Mysteries

In order to go into the interior of Africa, Europeans needed to explore and map the area, mainly the rivers, which were the primary means of transportation.

One of the most important and mysterious rivers was the Nile, the lifeblood of Egyptian civilization. It doesn't rain much in Egypt, so the yearly flood of the Nile provided all the water and rich soil needed to grow crops. Europeans and many others were curious about where the Nile River started.

The Lualaba was another major river that Europeans wanted to explore and map. Europeans wondered if it was part of the mighty Congo River that eventually emptied into the Atlantic Ocean. If so, it could be a way to transport goods from the interior to the coast of Africa.

Lake Victoria was another mystery. Was it one large lake or several smaller ones, as most people of the 1800's believed?

Of course, Europeans wanted to know about the terrain, climate, and people of interior Africa—were there mountains, thick jungles, lots of rain, food sources, friendly people? They needed as much information as they could get.

A few explorers had ventured into central Africa, but none had been able to bring back enough information to clear up all the mysteries. It would take a tough man from Wales to find the "treasure" of information about central Africa and its people.

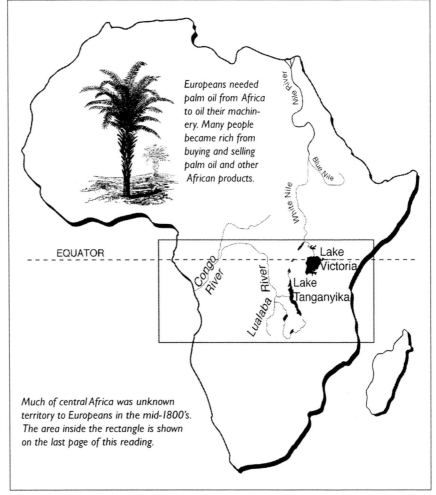

Europeans needed palm oil from Africa to oil their machinery. Many people became rich from buying and selling palm oil and other African products.

Much of central Africa was unknown territory to Europeans in the mid-1800's. The area inside the rectangle is shown on the last page of this reading.

Henry Morton Stanley

Henry Morton Stanley was born in Wales (now part of the United Kingdom) in 1841. He spent much of his life in a workhouse because none of his relatives wanted him. Workhouses were places run by the government where children, poor people, and sick people were forced to go if there was no one who would take care of them.

Years of hard work and loneliness in the workhouse made Stanley a very tough man, both mentally and physically.

Off to America

As a teenager with nothing to lose, Stanley ran away from the workhouse. He took a job on a ship that was going to America, where he became caught up in the American Civil War.

Even though he was not an American by birth, Stanley served with the Confederate Army, then with the Union Navy. His job in the navy was to write the ship's log. This experience gave him the idea to make writing his life's work. He sent some reports of Civil War battles to newspapers. The newspapers printed his stories.

After the Civil War, Henry worked as a reporter for the *Missouri Democrat* newspaper. Then he landed a job with the *New York Herald*. He was sent to Africa to report on a war in Abyssinia (present-day Ethiopia).

In 1869, the *Herald* sent him on one of his most famous assignments. He was to go to Africa and find Dr. Livingstone, an English missionary and explorer who had not been heard from in many years. This was Stanley's first expedition into Africa. He suffered from the heat and the insects. He hiked in knee-deep mud. He had spells of near-craziness from taking large amounts of quinine for the fevers caused by malaria. After much effort, he found Dr. Livingstone and asked the famous question, "Dr. Livingstone, I presume?" when he finally met the old man.

The world was amazed, and Henry Stanley became famous.

Quest to Explore Central Africa

After Livingstone's death in 1873, Henry Stanley vowed that he would continue Livingstone's exploration of Africa. He would also write about his adventures. Not only would he find the source of the Nile, but he would also explore the Lualaba River and areas of central Africa that were totally unknown to the

Henry Morton Stanley

outside world. Follow his expedition below and on the next two pages. The numbers in the story match numbers on the map on page 70 that show where Stanley's expedition was at that point in the story.

(1) *August 1874.* Stanley leaves England and arrives in Zanzibar. He has three river boats built. Supplies include guns, food, and medicine. He also takes beads, wire, and cloth to pay tribes for food along the way. Three hundred fifty-six Africans (including women and children), three Englishmen, and several dogs go with Stanley.

(2) *December 1874.* Stanley forces group to march quickly. Famine in area, difficult to get food; 20 people in expedition die, 89 run away.

(3) *January 1875.* Local tribes attack with spears, but Stanley forces group to continue. Only 166 people survive.

(4) *February 1875.* Stanley reaches Lake Victoria. Friendlier tribes here. Stanley hires 100 men.

(5) *March 1875.* Stanley and 11 crewmen start trip to sail around Lake Victoria.

(6) *April 1875.* With few problems, Stanley and crew reach kingdom of Uganda. Met by crowd of thousands. Stanley visits King Mtesa of Uganda. The people have rich clothes, many possessions, and a well-trained army. They have been influenced by Muslim traders and have converted to the Islamic religion. At this point, halfway around the lake, Stanley realizes that it is one big lake, rather than several small ones.

(7) Stanley continues trip around lake and reaches island of Bumbiri. The people attack and drag the boat ashore. Stanley fights the warriors with his elephant gun as his men push the boat back into the water and get away. Stanley vows revenge on the people of Bumbiri.

In November 1876 the expedition meets a friendly people, the Waregga, in the thick forest. Stanley noted that the Waregga treasured the skins of goats, mongoose, weasel, and leopards. They had well-made houses and furniture.

(8) *May 1875.* Stanley and crew finally reach base camp. Stanley has lost 73 pounds and 6 more men.

(9) *Winter 1875.* With canoes sent by King Mtesa, Stanley goes back to Uganda along the western side of the lake. He gets revenge on the Bumbiri people by attacking and killing 30 warriors.

(10) *March 1876.* Stanley and crew travel around Lake Tanganyika in 55 days, mapping the coastline and seeing no possibility that it could be the source of the Nile. He now strongly believes that Lake Victoria must be the source.

(11) *November 5, 1876.* Stanley marches into the most dangerous and least known part of Africa. He hires several hundred men from an Arab slave trader named Tippu Tib. The expedition begins fighting its way through the dense forest, "crawling, scrambling, tearing through the damp, dank jungles," according to Stanley's diary.

November 19, 1876. Stanley launches one boat into Lualaba River while most of the men are with Tippu Tib, marching along beside the river.

November 23, 1876. Drums beat. Shouts of "Ooh-hu-hu!" are heard from jungle, and the camp is attacked by 100 screaming tribesmen. Attackers are driven off. Smallpox, dysentery, typhoid fever, pneumonia, ulcers plague members of expedition; two or three bodies are thrown into river every day.

December 18, 1876. Rains begin. Expedition attacked by tribesmen with poison arrows; Stanley only has 30 men well enough to fight; they build a temporary stockade and somehow manage to fight off the attackers.

December 23, 1876. Tippu Tib and his men leave the expedition. With 20 captured canoes, Stanley and his group (now numbering 149) go on.

(12) *January 1877.* Attacks by tribesmen continue. The expedition passes through seven falls covering 50 miles (later named Stanley Falls). Most of the time they carry the canoes around the falls by cutting a path 15 feet wide through the jungle, fighting off warriors almost constantly.

(13) *January 27, 1877.* Past the falls, the boats are put into the river again. At this point the river curves to the west, so it is obviously part of the Congo River. For the next seven weeks the river is calm and wide, but the attacks continue.

(14) *February 1, 1877.* Stanley and crew attacked by 2,000 warriors in huge canoes. Stanley's guns overpower the attackers. Stanley and his men follow the tribesmen ashore. In a frenzy of revenge, they loot and plunder the village.

(15) *March 1877.* Almost at the point of starvation, the expedition reaches a part of the river that is like a large pool (later named Stanley Pool). The tribes there are friendly and willing to trade for food. They arrive at another set of falls. These falls have prevented all other Europeans from exploring the Congo.

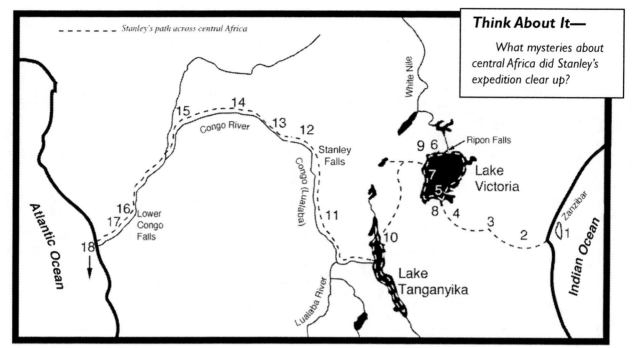

Think About It—

What mysteries about central Africa did Stanley's expedition clear up?

A young Arab who was with a caravan that tried to go into central Africa described to Stanley some of the dangers: "There is nothing but woods, and woods, and woods, for days, and weeks, and months." He told of cannibal warriors, huge boa constrictors, gorillas that bite your fingers off, and falls on the river that drown men.

(16) *March 28, 1877.* A canoe with a crew of eight men is swept over falls. All drown, including Kalulu, a boy that Stanley has come to think of as his "son."

(17) *Spring/Summer 1877.* Progress is slow; canoes must be carried over a mountain; some local tribesmen help.

(18) *August 9, 1877.* Expedition reaches Embomma, a major trading post near the coast. They have traveled 7,000 miles across Africa. Stanley and remaining crew board a sailing ship back to Zanzibar. Of 359 people who had started with Stanley, only 82 return. None of the other white men survives the trip. (None of the dogs survive, either.)

January 1878. Stanley arrives back in Europe. He is welcomed as a hero.

This drawing shows Mtesa, the king of Uganda, and some of his chiefs. Before Stanley arrived, Ugandans had already had contact with Arabs, who had converted Mtesa to the Islamic religion.

Name _____

Date _____

The Waregga — A Tribe of Central Africa in the 1870's

Henry Stanley led an expedition through central Africa that lasted from 1875 to 1877. He explored many areas, including the Congo River, and met many tribes never seen before by outsiders.

After "crawling, scrambling, tearing through the damp, dank jungles," Stanley and his group met the Waregga, who lived in a thick woods (or jungle) near the Congo River.

The following reading is taken from Stanley's diary, published in his book, *Through the Dark Continent* (London: George Newnes, Ltd., 1899). It describes what Stanley saw when he met the Waregga.

Fenced round by their seldom penetrated woods, the Waregga have hitherto led lives as secluded [hidden from outside world] as the troops of chimpanzees in their forest. Their villages consist of long rows of houses, all connected together in one block ... divided into several apartments for the respective families.

The roofs glisten as though smeared with coal-tar. There are shelves for fuel, and netting for swinging their crockery [cooking pots]; into the roof are thrust ... the pipe, and bunch of tobacco leaves, the stick of dried snails, various mysterious compounds wrapped in leaves of plants, pounded herbs, and what not. Besides these we noted, as household treasures, the skins of goats, mongoose or civet, weasel, wild cat, monkey, and leopard, shells of land snails, very large and prettily marked....

... over the door are also horns of goats and small forest deer, and ... the gaudy war head-

dress of feathers of the grey-bodied and crimson-tailed parrots, the drum, and some heavy broad-bladed spears with ironwood staffs.

Stanley also notices that the Waregga houses had furniture:

... in the depths of this forest of Uregga every family possessed a neatly made water-cane settee [small sofa], which would seat comfortably 3 persons.

Another very useful article of furniture was the bench 4 or 5 feet long, cut out of a single log of white soft wood....

Another noteworthy piece of furniture is the the fork of a tree, cut off where the branches begin to ramify [branch out]. This, when trimmed and peeled, is placed in an inverted position. The branches, sometimes 3 or even 4, serve as legs of a singular back-rest.

Stanley describes some of the dress of the Waregga:

All the adult males wear skull-caps of goat or monkey-skin, except the chief and elders, whose heads were covered with the aristocratic leopard-skin, with the tail of the leopard hanging down the back like a tassel.

The women were weighted with massive and bright iron rings. One of them, who was probably a lady of importance, carried at least 12 pounds of iron and 5 pounds of copper rings on her arms and legs....

(continued)

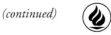

Name _____

Date _____

The Waregga — A Tribe of Central Africa in the 1870's *(continued)*

◆ *Objective:* To become familiar with a culture of central Africa in the 1870's

◆ *Time to Complete Activity:* About 2–4 hours

◆ *Materials Needed:* Index cards, glue stick, felt-tip pens, scissors, basket or box

Directions:

— A **culture kit** is a collection of cards and items that give information about a certain group of people and the way they live—for example, how they behave, their arts and beliefs, how they dress, how they build their houses, the animals they live near, etc.

— After reading Stanley's description of the Waregga people, make a culture kit for the Waregga.

— Using index cards, make at least five cards for the Waregga culture. Each card should have a description of some aspect of the culture and a picture that illustrates what is written on the card. A sample card is shown on this page. You can copy drawings from this chapter, from this page, or you can use your imagination. For instance, you could draw or copy a picture of an African woman and draw iron or copper rings on her arms and legs to show how Waregga women displayed their importance in their culture. (This was how Stanley interpreted the rings.)

— Make an "artifact" to include in the culture kit. This can be a small model of something from the culture—clothing, furniture, headdress, jewelry, etc. In the case of the Waregga, for instance, you could try to find a small, forked tree limb, turn it upside down, and make a Waregga backrest, like the one Stanley describes.

— Organize your cards and "artifact" in a basket or box for others to enjoy.

Variation: Make a map card for the culture kit showing the area of central Africa where the Waregga were living when Stanley and his expedition met them in 1876 (close to where the Lualaba River becomes the Congo River).

Variation: Make a culture kit for a group of people who live in central Africa today—in the Democratic Republic of Congo, Uganda, Kenya, or Tanzania. (These countries include some of the areas that Stanley's expedition traveled through in the 1870's.)

Waregga Spear

Settee—Waregga People of Central Africa, 1870's

The Waregga used a low settee, made of water cane. This was like a sofa that three people could sit on. The settee was made by weaving stems of the water-cane plant.

Name _____

Date _____

Animals of Central Africa, 1870's and Now

Henry Stanley led an expedition through central Africa that lasted from 1874 to 1877. He explored many areas, including the Congo River, and met many tribes never seen before by outsiders. Below are some of the animals that Stanley wrote about in his diary during this expedition. The animals are listed according to the area in which Stanley saw them or heard about them from Africans. The numbers on the list match the numbers on the map.

(1) giraffe, hycna, zebra, buffalo, antelope (In his diary, Stanley writes about shooting zebra for meat.)

(2) lion, leopard, otter, two-horned rhinoceros (Stanley shoots rhinoceros for meat.)

(3) crocodile, hippopotamus

(4) mongoose, weasel, wildcat, monkey (white-necked, glossy black, and small gray), leopard, parrots, python, green viper, puff adder, lemur, baboon, chimpanzee

- ◆ *Objective:* To become aware of animals that lived in central Africa in the 1870's and whether or not they have become endangered in modern times
- ◆ *Time to Complete Activity:* Probably 2–4 hours over several weeks, depending on research involved
- ◆ *Materials Needed:* Poster board, scissors, felt-tip pens, glue stick, resource books and materials, access to copy machine

Directions:

___ Enlarge the map on this page on a copier.

— Cut the map out and glue it onto poster board.

— Find and copy pictures of as many animals as you can from the list to the left.

— Glue the animal pictures on the poster board around the map. Group them according to the area where Stanley and his expedition saw these animals or heard about them. Number the groups 1 to 4. Draw lines from the groups to the same numbered areas.

— Research whether these animals are endangered in modern times. If so, indicate it on the poster by drawing a circle around that animal.

— Display your poster and research for others to see.

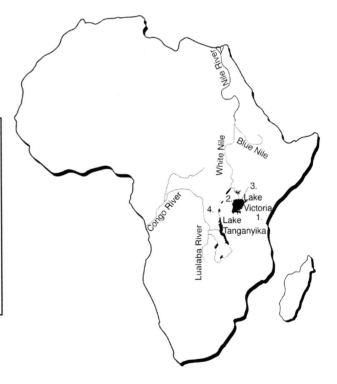

Name _____

Date _____

Thought/Discussion Questions

1. Why do you think Stanley and the people in his expedition were able to fight off so many attacking warriors? What was the main advantage that Stanley and his group had?

   _____

   _____

   _____

   _____

2. What kind of qualities do you think an explorer of Africa in the 1870's needed to succeed? Do you have those qualities?

   _____

   _____

   _____

3. Do you think Stanley and other Europeans had the "right" or "duty" to explore central Africa? Please explain.

   _____

   _____

   _____

4. Do you know from other readings, or can you guess, what happened after central Africa was explored by Europeans?

   _____

   _____

   _____

   _____

CHAPTER 8: *Gold Brings a Clash of Cultures in Southern Africa*

Chapter Summary

What is the "wonder" in this story?

- Gold was discovered in 1886 in the Transvaal Republic of southern Africa.

What are the major themes about South Africa and its people in this chapter?

- The Dutch Boers who came to southern Africa starting in the 1600's were a tough and fiercely independent people, determined to keep the homeland they had fought for.
- The British who first came to southern Africa in 1798 were also determined to control southern Africa, including the Boer republics.

- The huge number of people who came to the goldfields of Transvaal in the late 1800's came into conflict with the ultraconservative Boer government of the Transvaal.
- From the time that white people came to southern Africa in the 1600's until the country of South Africa's first election by universal suffrage in 1994, native Africans' civil and human rights were denied.

Answer to "Think About It" Question

(page 81)

Under the South African system of segregation called "apartheid," black South Africans by law were not allowed to marry whites, ride on buses or trains with them, stay in the same hotels, or take skilled jobs reserved for whites. They were required to carry a government pass to travel from one area of the country to another. Starting in 1978, many of these restrictions were lifted, but blacks still could not vote and they could not go to the same schools or hospitals as whites.

In 1985, the South African government declared a countrywide emergency, and police started roaming the black communities, hurting and killing thousands of black South Africans. The government tried to conceal these actions by not letting radio, television, or newspaper reporters see what was happening.

In 1986, the United States and other countries protested South Africa's racial policies by not lending money to the South African government and not allowing certain goods to be sold to South Africa.

Under worldwide pressure, in 1990 Nelson Mandela, a black political leader who had been in prison for 28 years for his actions against the government, was released. Other political prisoners were also released. Apartheid laws were lifted.

In 1994 all South Africans, black and white, voted in a general election. Nelson Mandela was elected president. Things have improved for black South Africans, but because they suffered under apartheid for so long, they have a long way to go before they are equal to whites in education, ability to get jobs, housing, and all other areas of life.

Answers to "Planning a New City"

(page 82)

These are some of the businesses and services that opened up in Johannesburg soon after the founding of the city in 1886:

banks

churches and a synagogue

schools

hospital (The first one could only handle 30 patients at a time.)

ice house (There were no refrigerators yet.)

lights (In 1889 the first electric power plant was started.)

telephones (Telephone lines and exchanges were connected in 1894.)

saloons

post office

theater

stock exchange

hotels

food market

Answers to "Thought/Discussion" Questions

(page 85)

1. Discussion ideas will vary.

Bibliography

Adult Books

Leach, Graham. *South Africa.* London: Routledge & Kegan Paul, 1986.

Morris, Jean, and Eleanor Preston-Whyte. *Speaking with Beads: Zulu Arts from Southern Africa.* New York: Thames and Hudson, 1994.

Rosenthal, Eric. *Gold! Gold! Gold! The Johannesburg Gold Rush.* New York: Macmillan, 1970.

Taylor, Stephen. *Shaka's Children: A History of the Zulu People.* London: HarperCollins, 1994.

Tessendorf, K.C. *Along the Road to Soweto: A Racial History of South Africa.* New York: Atheneum, 1989.

Juvenile Books

Angelou, Maya. (Photographs by Margaret Courtney-Clarke) *My Painted House, My Friendly Chicken, and Me.* New York: Clarkson Potter, 1994. (Picture book of life in an Ndebele village of South Africa)

Coombs, Charles. *Gold and Other Precious Metals.* New York: William Morrow, 1981.

Meltzer, Milton. *Gold: The True Story of Why People Search for It, Mine It, Trade It, Steal It, Mint It, Hoard It, Shape It, Wear It, Fight and Kill for It.* New York: HarperCollins, 1993.

Smith, Chris. *Conflict in Southern Africa.* New York: New Discovery Books, 1993.

CHAPTER 8:
Gold Brings a Clash of Cultures in Southern Africa

AFRICA

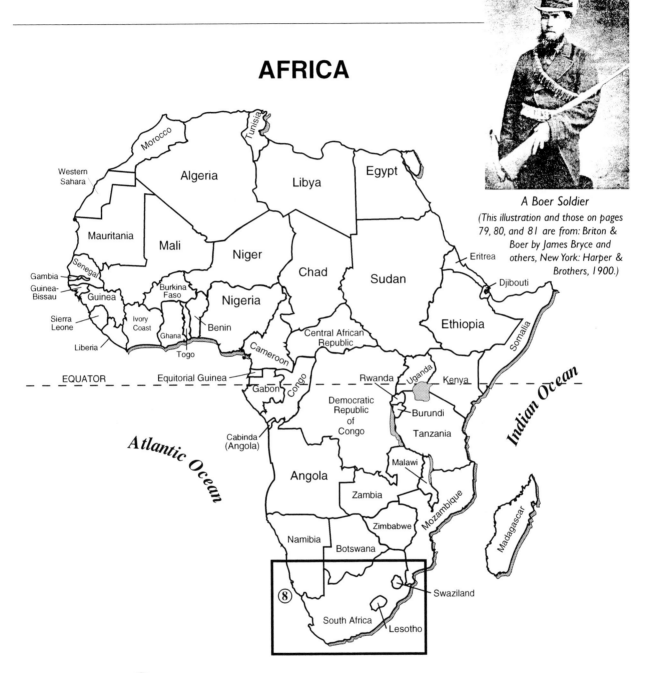

A Boer Soldier
(This illustration and those on pages 79, 80, and 81 are from: Briton & Boer by James Bryce and others, New York: Harper & Brothers, 1900.)

(8) The focus of this chapter is the 1886 gold rush of southern Africa.

Europeans Settle in Southern Africa

Beginning in the 1600's, people from the Netherlands started coming to live in southern Africa. They founded Cape Town.

In 1798, England received southern Africa as a prize of war in Europe, and the English took over Cape Town.

At the time of the great gold discoveries in southern Africa in 1886, England controlled several areas, and Boers,* farmers from the Netherlands, controlled several other areas (as shown on the map, below). There was no country called "South Africa."

Many of the native people had been killed as whites sought to settle southern Africa. Many worked as laborers or servants for the white settlers. Other groups of native Africans lived near the white settlers and often fought with them.

Areas inhabited by two of the largest native groups, the Xhosa and the Zulu, are shown on the map. Lesotho, home of the Basotho people, and Swaziland, home of the Swazi people, were also native African population centers. These two areas eventually became independent countries.

The native black Africans always outnumbered whites in southern Africa (and still do).

---

* "Boer" means "farmer" in the Dutch language.

A "Tail" of Gold

In February 1886, George Walker, who had come from England to look for gold, was near Pretoria in southern Africa. He reported that he was walking across a field of tall grass when he noticed an outcrop of bare rock sticking out of the ground. He got his gold-mining pan, broke off a piece of the soft rock, and crushed it. As gold miners have done for centuries, he mixed the rock in the pan with water and swirled it around. As he watched excitedly, the lighter parts of the rock were washed away, leaving behind the heavier "tail" of gold sparking in the sun.

Later, Walker and a friend named George Harrison signed a prospecting contract with the owner of

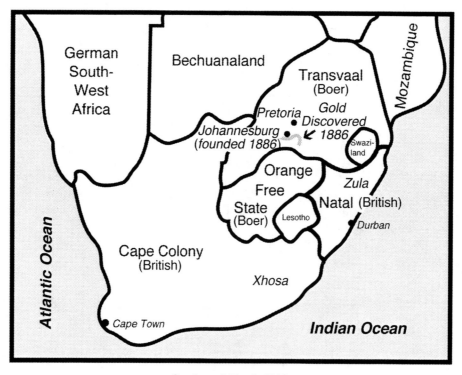

Southern Africa in 1886

the land where the gold was found. The two Georges did not suspect that the gold they would dig up would be the beginning of the richest gold strike in history.

Diggers, Diggers, and More Diggers

After word got out about Walker's discovery, people came to southern Africa in huge numbers from all over the world. "Newcomers turned up every day, by ox wagon, by horse wagon, by mule wagon, and by every imaginable sort of vehicle . . ." reported a doctor named Hans Sauer. (Rosenthal, p. 139.)

The farms owned by local Boers began to be overrun by people looking for gold.

Rough mining camps sprang up. People lived in tents, wagons, and sometimes in primitive shacks made of reeds and clay.

Men who were already rich were buying up large parcels of gold-rich farmland that would make them even richer. One farm was purchased from a widow for about $7,500. Gold from the mines on the farm eventually totaled between 100 million and 200 million British pounds.

Deep Gold

Only a small portion of the gold was on top of the ground. Most of it was buried deep, in layers of rock. Long shafts had to be dug to get to the rock. When the rock was brought up, it had to be crushed to free the gold.

Super-rich Randlord Cecil Rhodes

The Randlords of Johannesburg thought the Boer government of the Transvaal was treating them unfairly by making them pay taxes but not giving them the right to vote. They had to live in Johannesburg 10 years before they could become citizens! The Randlords did, however, agree with the Boers about how to treat the native black workers: pay them low wages and give them practically no rights at all.

At first, individual diggers, black and white, could stake out small claims, dig trenches, and take out some gold. But eventually, companies with money to buy expensive digging and rock-crushing equipment pushed out individuals. The owners of these mines were known as Randlords, because the gold was discovered in a region of Transvaal called the Witwatersrand. Most Randlords were British.

Men came from all over the world to work in the gold mines. Many native Africans were hired as laborers for much less money than whites were paid.

Boomtown!

Almost overnight the town of Johannesburg sprang up on the Witwatersrand, near the goldfields.

Within several years, temporary houses of canvas had been replaced by sturdy houses made of brick and stone. Money from Rand gold had built a city with a telegraph office, a hospital, a fire station, a courthouse, newspapers, a large vegetable market, and of course, banks and a stock exchange. So many people crowded into the hotels that some had to sleep in the dining rooms, billiard rooms, and entrances.

One type of business that Johannesburg had plenty of was saloons, or bars. In about 1889 the Crystal Palace, the Elephant and Castle, and Diggers' Arms were just a few of the colorful names given the 127 saloons serving just 20,000 people, mostly men.

Boers versus Uitlanders (Foreigners)

The Boers of the Transvaal had fought hard for their land. They had defeated black tribesmen in the area and fought off the British, who wanted the Transvaal to be under their control.

When gold was discovered near Pretoria, the Boers were living apart from other people. They had very few roads and limited communication with the

Starting in 1834, Boer farmers and their families started moving away from the Cape Town area to escape English control. These "trekkers," as they called themselves, were tough and very independent. Each family owned a covered wagon, pulled by teams of oxen and driven by native servants. When the trekkers were attacked by Matabele warriors, they would tie the wagons together in a square and stuff the openings with thorny brush. With their guns, the Boers could usually hold off the spear-carrying warriors, who did not have guns. When the trekkers came to a place that they wanted to call home, their wagons became their first houses (see drawing, above).

outside world. There were only about 40,000 of them living as farmers or ranchers.

The Boers were very strict in their religious beliefs. They thought that many people in Johannesburg lived in an ungodly way with their drinking in the saloons, horse racing, and prizefighting. The Boers were afraid that these Uitlanders would corrupt their children.

Boer president Paul Kruger expressed this fear of Uitlanders when he said bluntly, "I am glad to hear of the coming of good people but will cut the throat of the bad ones."

By 1890, Johannesburg had grown bigger than Pretoria. The Uitlanders asked many things from the Boers, including the right to vote and better schools.

The Boer War

Pressures began to build between the Uitlanders and the Boers. Great Britain decided that the two Boer republics, the Transvaal and the Orange Free State, must come under British control. The Boers were determined to remain independent.

The two Boer republics went to war with Britain in October 1899. President Kruger stated, "The republics are determined, if they must belong to England, that a price will be paid that will stagger humanity."

In the beginning of the war the Boers won many battles, because they knew the land much better than the British. Also, Boer sharpshooters on horseback had the advantage over the British, who blundered around dragging heavy cannons.

After British soldiers sailed from England to join their troops in southern Africa, overwhelming numbers (about 500,000 British to about 88,000 Boers) helped the British start winning the war. They entered Johannesburg in May 1900, and soon took over Pretoria.

Boer forces refused to give up. They began a guerrilla war in which they struck at the British in small groups. To end the war, the British began burning the Boer houses and food supplies and putting the women and children into camps. Disease broke out in the camps, and about 28,000 Boers died, mostly children.

Neither the British nor the Boers would allow native Africans to fight. Instead, they were used to dig trenches, carry supplies, string barbed-wire fences, and dig graves. About 14,000 Africans also died in the British camps.

Finally, the exhausted Boers gave up the fight and signed a peace treaty in May 1902. They agreed to become part of a country controlled by Britain. Eight years later, South Africa became a self-governing country within the British Empire.

Although they were defeated in war, the Boers still kept their traditions and their language, called Afrikaans (developed from Dutch of the 1600's). The people descended from the Boers, or Afrikaners, eventually outnumbered the British and became leaders of the South African government.

In the new country of South Africa, native black Africans had very limited civil rights and were forced to live separately from whites.

Johannesburg is now a large metropolitan city with a population of several million. The older gold mines have given out, but the goldfields still produce about 30 million ounces of gold a year!

> ### Think About It—
>
> *Do you remember from news reports or articles you have read about some of the changes that have happened in South Africa in the 1990's, especially changes for black South Africans?*

The spears and arrows of native Africans, such as this proud Matabele warrior, were no match for the rifles of the British

Name _____

Date _____

Planning a New City

The city of Johannesburg sprang up almost overnight after gold was discovered in 1886 near Pretoria, in southern Africa.

The first plan for Johannesburg laid out a village of 600 lots along a 75-foot-wide main street, with side streets 70 feet wide.

Soon, many businesses and services started up to support the thousands of gold miners who came to Johannesburg to seek their fortune.

◆ *Objective:* To have the experience of deciding what businesses and services are necessary to support the people who live in a city
◆ *Time to Complete Activity:* About 1 hour
◆ *Materials Needed:* This sheet, pen or pencil

This is Johannesburg 10 years after it was founded. (Illustration from: South Africa: Its History, Heroes and Wars, by W. Douglas MacKenzie, Chicago: Monarch Book Co., 1899.)

Directions:

___ List as many businesses and services you can think of that would spring up to support the new city of Johannesburg. Remember, this is a town of the late 1800's.

_____

_____

_____

_____

_____

_____

_____

_____

_____

_____

_____

_____

Name _____

Date _____

Making a Traditional Zulu Beadwork Design

The Zulu people of southern Africa live mainly in the Natal region. For a very long time they have used colorful beads to decorate their head coverings and clothing. Once, all Zulus wore beadwork. Now, the only Zulus who wear beads are those who live in rural areas and still worship their ancestors rather than following the Christian religion brought to the area by white missionaries.

Not only do the beads show a desire to follow traditional ways, including ancestor worship, but they also show if the wearer is male or female, married or single, and what part of Natal he or she comes from.

For instance, only men and unmarried women from the Nongoma area, in northern Natal, wear strips of beading crossing the chest and going over the shoulders.

In many areas, married women wear leather skirts with beaded aprons.

In an area near Durban, men who are dancing in festivals wear animal skins and feathers, beaded anklets and arm bands. In this same festival, girls who are too young to marry wear short red skirts, beaded aprons, and no headbands. Girls who are ready to get married wear short black skirts with beading and headbands. Married women dance in longer black skirts with beaded aprons and head coverings decorated with broad bands of beadwork. They also carry umbrellas and small shields as they dance.

Traditional Zulus believe that the ancestors give certain people powers to "see" why someone is sick, to find something that is lost, and to tell the future. These people, called diviners, wear long headdresses of white or multicolored beads.

◆ *Objective:* To make a traditional Zulu beadwork design
◆ *Time to Complete Activity:* About 1 hour
◆ *Materials Needed:* This sheet, colored pencils or pens, access to copier, if desired

---

Directions:

___ Follow the directions below to complete a beadwork design in the traditional colors.

For top design:

◆ The diamond shape on the inside of the design starts with green in the middle, then black, white, red, and green again. Continue this pattern of colors.

◆ The triangle shapes on the sides start with white in the larger area, then a red strip, then green, black, and white again. Continue this pattern of colors.

◆ The zigzag shapes start with black in the smallest area, then green, red, and white. Continue this pattern of colors.

For bottom design:

◆ The head of the girl shape is black.
◆ The shoulders are red with green triangles.
◆ The middle triangle is black.
◆ The bottom triangle is red.
◆ The feet and legs are black.
◆ The rectangle shapes are red, green, and black stripes.

Variation: Cut out one of the designs, enlarge it on a copier, color it, and use it as a design on a book cover, a cover for a research project, etc.

Variation: Copy one of the designs onto graph paper and use it as a cross-stitch or needlepoint design.

(continued)

Making a Traditional Zulu Beadwork Design *(continued)*

This is a diamond-shaped pattern of Nongoma beadwork. The Zulu believe the shape represents a shield that protects the wearer from harm.

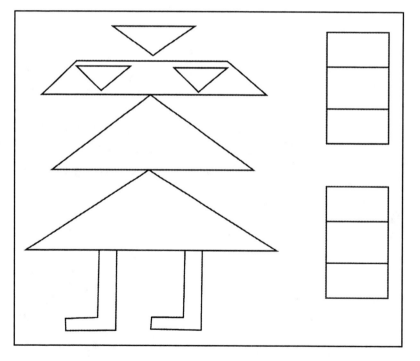

This design represents a girl without a head covering. The design would be used in beadwork worn by girls and unmarried men.

Name _____

Date _____

Thought/Discussion Questions

Until recently, black South Africans suffered under a system of segregation called **apartheid**, an Afrikaans word that means "kept apart." Apartheid laws stopped blacks from riding trains and buses with whites, from taking jobs reserved for whites, and required them to have a government pass to travel from one area of the country to another. The following poem was written by a black South African who lives in Soweto, a group of black communities near Johannesburg. During apartheid, black South Africans could work in Johannesburg but were forbidden to live there. Instead, they lived in the poor and violent environment of Soweto, where white police crushed any sign of rebellion. After reading the poem, discuss what you think life was like for people in Soweto. Definitions for some of the words are given on the bottom of the page.

Nightfall in Soweto

Nightfall comes like
a dreaded disease
seeping through the pores
of a healthy body
and ravaging[1] it beyond repair.

A murderer's hand,
lurking in the shadows,
clasping the dagger,
strikes down the helpless victim.

I am the victim.
I am slaughtered
every night in the streets.
I am cornered by the fear
gnawing at my timid heart;
in my helplessness I languish[2].

Man has ceased to be man
Man has become beast
Man has become prey[3].

I am the prey;
I am the quarry[4] to be run down
by the marauding[5] beast
let loose by cruel nightfall
from his cage of death.

Where is my refuge?
Where am I safe?
Not in my matchbox house
Where I barricade[6] myself against nightfall.

I tremble at his crunching footsteps,
I quake at his deafening knock at the door.
"Open up!" he barks like a rabid[7] dog
thirsty for my blood.

Nightfall! Nightfall!
You are my mortal enemy.
But why were you ever created?
Why can't it be daytime?
Daytime forever more?

—*Oswald Mbuyiseni Mtshali*

[1] destroying
[2] become weak, lose my strength
[3] animal that is hunted down for food
[4] prey
[5] searching for something to steal or hurt
[6] locking the doors, locking the windows so no one can get in
[7] sick and crazy

Share Your Bright Ideas with Us!

We want to hear from you! Your valuable comments and suggestions will help us meet your current and future classroom needs.

Your name_____Date_____

School name_____Phone_____

School address_____

Grade level taught_____Subject area(s) taught_____Average class size_____

Where did you purchase this publication?_____

Was your salesperson knowledgeable about this product?   Yes_____   No_____

What monies were used to purchase this product?

___School supplemental budget   ___Federal/state funding   ___Personal

Please "grade" this Walch publication according to the following criteria:

Quality of service you received when purchasing	A	B	C	D	F
Ease of use	A	B	C	D	F
Quality of content	A	B	C	D	F
Page layout	A	B	C	D	F
Organization of material	A	B	C	D	F
Suitability for grade level	A	B	C	D	F
Instructional value	A	B	C	D	F

COMMENTS:_____

_____

What specific supplemental materials would help you meet your current—or future—instructional needs?

_____

Have you used other Walch publications? If so, which ones?_____

May we use your comments in upcoming communications?   ___Yes   ___No

Please **FAX** this completed form to **207-772-3105**, or mail it to:

Product Development, J. Weston Walch, Publisher, P.O. Box 658, Portland, ME 04104-0658

We will send you a **FREE GIFT** as our way of thanking you for your feedback. **THANK YOU!**